little India
at home

little India® at home

Photography by Sean Shadbolt

PENGUIN BOOKS

INTRODUCTION

Little India is a chain of restaurants that spans New Zealand from Auckland to Invercargill. All the recipes we use come from our grandmother, Premjit Kaur Gill, who trains Little India's head chefs in her kitchen in Chandigarh, India. When you come to Little India we want you to feel as if you have come into our home and you are trying our family recipes. The inspiration to write this cookbook was to give you the opportunity to recreate those recipes in your own home.

The recipes in this book have been adapted from our restaurant kitchen to be cooked in your home kitchen. In our Little India restaurants we use traditional tandoor ovens with a clay pot that are fired by charcoal, not gas, unlike many other Indian restaurants in New Zealand. The clay pot and the charcoal give our dishes and breads their great flavour. Because most people do not have a tandoor oven at home we have adapted our recipes so you can achieve a similar delicious result in your kitchen.

There is a perception that Indian food is complex, with so many different ingredients and cooking methods. In this book we have tried to make our recipes easy for everyone to achieve, whether you are a first-time cook or a bit of a whiz in the kitchen.

It is a good idea to read our recipes in full before you start so you'll know how much time you need for preparation and have all the ingredients on hand. If there's any spice or ingredient mentioned that you haven't heard of before, check the Indian Pantry section (pages 18–23) for an explanation.

If you have not tried Little India food before then please head to our website www.littleindia.co.nz and book your table or place a takeaway or delivery order – and then use this book to recreate the experience in your kitchen!

THE LITTLE INDIA STORY

The story of Little India begins with Sukhmohan Singh Gill (Sukhi), who was born in Jodhpur, Rajasthan. After graduating from school in 1972, he helped his parents build their family home in New Delhi and was then sent to England for further studies. He was to become an accountant. Two years later he met his wife-to-be, Joanna, in Worchester, England. At the time Sukhi was still studying accounting and Joanna was working as a chef. They married in 1982. After living in England together for several years they decided to move to New Zealand. Sukhi's older sister Sukhinder was already living in New Zealand and told them Dunedin was a great place to live and bring up children.

So Sukhi, Joanna and their family moved to Dunedin in 1986. Sukhi initially worked as an accountant, but felt that pursuing an accounting career in New Zealand was not for him. In 1987 he decided to go into business for himself, so he could be his own boss, and bought a dairy

This page, from top to bottom: Sukhi Gill, the founder of Little India, aged seven (1962); Sukhi's mother, Premjit Kaur Gill, on her honeymoon in South India (1948); group protest seeking independence from British rule in India (1946).

Opposite: Sukhi's grandfather, Sardar Surmukh Singh, in Agra (1948).

in Ravensbourne, Dunedin. The dairy also had a fish and chip shop attached to it, which Sukhi saw as an added bonus because it brought more people to the dairy. About a year after he opened the business, Sukhi's father, Jasbir, and mother, Premjit (who now live in Chandigarh, in the Punjab region of North India), came to visit. Sukhi asked Premjit, with Joanna's help, to cook a curry that he could sell in the fish and chip shop as a special. This sold out very quickly so he asked Premjit to make another one the next night. Again it sold out! Word got around that great Indian food was available in Ravensbourne, and soon there were people from all over Dunedin lining up for curry on the weekends. Little did the customers know that the curry was being made on an electric stovetop cooker in Sukhi and Joanna's kitchen above the dairy.

Continued on page 13

This page, from top to bottom: members of the District Inspecting Staff & Headmaster of High Schools, with Sukhi's grandfather, Surmukh Singh, in the second row (1927); Sukhi's father, Squadron Leader Jasbir Singh Gill, and crew waiting for the Dakota DC-3 to be refuelled to transport aeroplane spare parts from the UK back to India (1950); as above.

Family photo taken in Agra during a visit from Sukhi's grandmother, Nihal Kaur, featuring Nihal, Jasbir and Premjit in the back row (left to right), and Shammi, Jugnu, Sukhi and Sukhinder in the front row (left to right) (1959).

Sukhi would have to shout up the stairs for his mother and Joanna to hurry up when things got busy, because if there were delays he would give away free soft drinks to the customers.

As things got busier and demand increased for Indian food at their fish and chip shop, Sukhi and Joanna decided that it was time to open an Indian restaurant. They sold the dairy and signed a lease to open their first Little India restaurant on St Andrew Street in Dunedin. Although Joanna had worked as a chef before, neither she nor Sukhi had any idea about how to run an Indian restaurant. This was a big risk to take, but Sukhi saw the demand for Indian food and decided to go for it. A family friend, Manjit Gujral, owned an Indian restaurant in Sydney so Sukhi got in touch with him. He was told, 'If you want to own an Indian restaurant, you need to work in a professionally run Indian kitchen. You have to be able to cook and create dishes yourself, without relying on your chefs.' So Sukhi went to Sydney for six weeks and spent most of his time in the kitchen working with the chefs. His first job was skinning chicken thigh fillets and learning some tandoori marinades. He was also put in charge of peeling and dicing the onions – his least favourite job. Once the chefs gained some confidence in his abilities he was allowed to cook the staff dinner on Tuesday nights. He still had some liberties while working in his friend's restaurant – a scotch was delivered to him every night at 9.30pm. To this day Sukhi is extremely grateful for his time and training in Sydney with Manjit Gujral and his family. It is a big gesture for any restaurateur to open up the doors of their business – especially the kitchen – for someone else to learn the trade.

Once Sukhi returned to Dunedin, the final work was done on the restaurant fit-out and Little India's doors opened on 4 July 1991. The name Little India was chosen by Sukhi and Joanna for the simple reason that the actual restaurant was small but India is such a vast country, and in that little space they would be bringing a taste of India to the public. While Sukhi and Joanna both liked the name, their family and friends were not convinced, but the couple went with their gut feeling.

The restaurant was very busy for the first three months and then suddenly business died down. Sukhi and Joanna were determined not to give up so they closed the restaurant to refine their recipes and decided to change from serving the food out of bain-maries to à la carte dining. During that time their chef left, so the recipes created by Sukhi and Joanna were all written out and stuck above the exhaust hoods so the new chef would be able to follow the recipes and make sure they were consistent.

Continued on page 17

This page: Sukhi outside the first Little India restaurant on St Andrews Street, Dunedin (1991).

Opposite, from top to bottom: the Gill family in Chandigarh (1965); Sukhi's father, Jasbir (second row, second from the right), during his second year at Punjab Agriculture University (1940).

Following, clockwise from top left: Sukhi's father, Jasbir, at Leh Airport in Kashmir, where they had to land on metal strips as there was no runway (1962); Sukhi's grandmother, Nihal Kaur, and mother, Premjit, in the back row (left to right) and Sukhi, Sukhinder, Shammi and Jugnu in the front row (left to right), in Delhi (1959); Premjit after her wedding to Sukhi's father, Jasbir (1948); Premjit playing a sitar in Jodhpur (1953); the family in Chandigarh with cousins and Nihal Kaur outside the house of Sukhi's uncle, Ranjit Singh Gill (1965).

400 MILES To INDIA
To CHINA 190 MILES

148

Sukhi's uncle Ranjit Singh, grandmother Nihal Kaur, uncle Bikram Singh, grandfather Sardar Surmukh and father Jasbir in the back row (left to right), with Sukhi's uncle Charanjit Singh in the front, Punjab (c. 1933).

In the early days the routine involved Joanna waking up and taking the children to school before going to the restaurant to clean up from the night before. Then she started on the prep work. Sukhi would come into the restaurant around 11am and help. The chef in training would arrive around 1pm to take over from Joanna, who would leave at 2pm to go and pick up the children from school. Sukhi would be at the restaurant until the early hours of the morning. Running the restaurant involved many long hours and hard work to begin with.

As time went on the restaurant got busier and more chefs were required. Sukhi rang his parents in Chandigarh and told them he needed more chefs. His father went to the local Indian restaurants to see the talent that was there. He then shortlisted some of the chefs and brought them home so his wife, Premjit, could check their skills. Word went around Chandigarh that there was an opportunity to go to New Zealand to work and chefs showed up on a daily basis to drop off their CVs at the family home. This still happens today.

The second Little India opened in Queenstown in 1993. At the time there were no real plans to open a second restaurant or for any big expansion; however, people travelling to Dunedin from Queenstown would come into Little India and say to Sukhi, 'When are you opening in Queenstown? We need a Little India there.' Again, Sukhi saw an opportunity and a gap in the market and went for it. This was also how a third restaurant opened in Merivale, Christchurch, in 1996. People kept asking Sukhi to open a Little India there – so he did.

A year later, Little India opened in Wellington. Sukhi's brother Jugnu was already involved in the business and he moved to Wellington to open the restaurant. Jugnu now owns five Little India restaurants across Wellington.

Twenty-two years after the first Little India opened, there are now seventeen Little India restaurants in New Zealand. The original dishes are still on our menu today, although the menu has expanded over the years. Premjit still trains and tests the chefs that Little India hires in her own kitchen in Chandigarh before they make the trip over to New Zealand to work. The core values and ingredients of the family recipes are taught to the new chefs. This is what the business was built on. Premjit's influence is still as strong today as it was in 1991, when the first Little India restaurant opened.

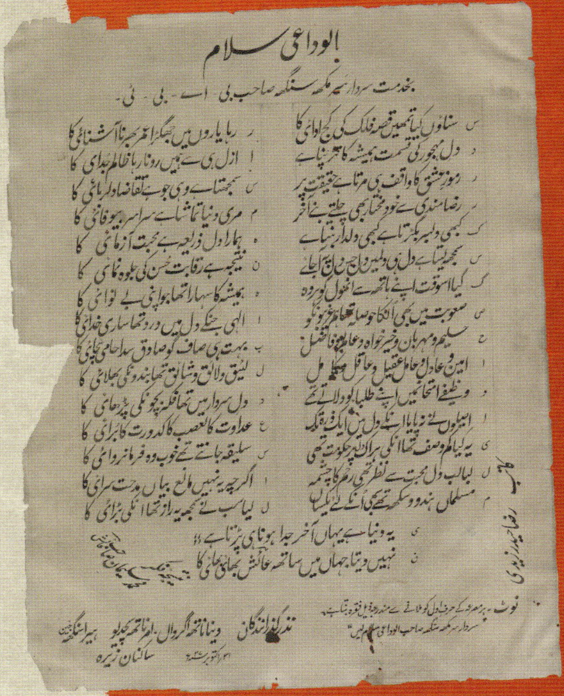

الوداعی سلام

بخدمت سردار سرمکھ سنگھ صاحب بی۔ اے۔ بی۔ ٹی۔

This page, from top to bottom: a speech written in Urdu by the staff of Sukhi's grandfather Surmukh, to farewell him when he retired as principal of Nathana School in Punjab, Delhi (1940); Sukhi's brother Jugnu (1961).

INDIAN PANTRY

A lot of people tell us that they would love to be able to cook Indian food at home but it is too hard. When you have a little bit of inside knowledge, this is not the case. Most Indian dishes consist of the same base of ingredients: onions, ginger, garlic and tomatoes. When you add different spices, herbs, meats and vegetables you can create a vast amount of dishes with different flavours and textures. In this section we will take you through the most commonly used of these ingredients so that you will not find the thought of cooking curry so daunting. You will need the ingredients in this section and more to make the recipes in our cookbook.

SPICES AND HERBS

You can buy spices from your local Indian supermarket but most are available at normal supermarkets. It is best to store spices in a cool place out of direct sunlight. Spices should be stored in an airtight container to preserve their freshness and flavour.

Black Pepper (Kali Mirch)

Black pepper effectively wards off colds and throat infections. We prefer to use whole black peppercorns in our dishes as they give a more intense and even flavour when they are cooked through the dish.

Carom Seeds (Ajwain)

We use carom seeds in our seafood dishes as we love the way they complement the flavours. Carom seeds are well known for their health benefits, helping with everything from indigestion to asthma.

Chaat Masala

Chaat masala is a seasoning that complements a variety of food. In India people use it for seasoning things like tandoori chicken and even fresh fruit. Chaat masala has a very zingy, tangy flavour and goes well with our starters. It can be bought at Indian supermarkets.

Chana Masala

Chana masala is a spice blend made to go with chickpea dishes. It adds zing to the dish and usually consists of coriander, green chilli, black pepper, mango powder and cumin seeds, as well as other additions. Chana masala can be bought at Indian supermarkets.

Cinnamon (Dalchini)

Cinnamon has a very distinct flavour and is used in savoury and sweet dishes. It has many health benefits and is said to help fight diabetes.

Cloves (Laung)

Cloves have a very strong flavour and come from a dried flower bud. They can help control tooth and gum infections, relieve nausea, combat colds, strengthen nerves and improve circulation.

Coriander (Dhaniya)

We occasionally use fresh coriander when cooking our dishes but more often as a garnish.

Cumin Seeds (Jeera)

Cumin seeds can be found in many different cuisines such as Indian, Mediterranean, Mexican and Middle Eastern. It is a good digestive to settle a heavy meal.

Dhansak Masala

This is a blend of spices made for a dhansak curry. At Little India we make Lamb Dhansak. Dhansak masala is usually a blend of turmeric, mustard seeds, fenugreek seeds, dried red chillies, cinnamon and cumin seeds. You can find ready-made dhansak masala in most Indian supermarkets.

Fenugreek (Kasoori Methi)

Fenugreek is made from the leaves of the plant, which are dried and ground. It has a very earthy flavour with a slightly bitter taste.

Garam Masala

Garam masala is the main spice used in our cooking. It is a mix of ground spices with intense flavour. It is not usually spicy but gives a warming sensation and flavour.

Green Cardamom (Elaichi)

Green cardamom pods have a very unusual and intense flavour. You do not need to use many pods to incorporate their flavour in your dish. Cardamom is said to help prevent kidney stones.

Paprika

Paprika is made from dried red capsicums that have been ground to a fine consistency. We use paprika to give our chicken dishes their orange colour, and it is also used in all of our lamb dishes.

Red Chilli Powder (Laal Mirch)

Red chilli powder is used to spice up our dishes. It is made from dried red chillies that are ground to a fine consistency. There are many different types of chilli powder that have different spice levels and can sometimes be made with blends of different chillies and other spices.

Salt (Namak)

Salt is used in our cooking to help bring out the flavours of our dishes. Too much salt can completely spoil a dish, but not enough salt and you will not taste the balance of flavours. We like to use less salt to start with and then add salt during the cooking process according to taste.

Turmeric (Haldi)

Turmeric is yellow in colour and does not have a strong flavour. It comes from the same plant family as ginger. Turmeric is said to be a blood purifier, boost liver function, prevent coughs and colds and improve skin tone. It is also an antiseptic.

White Pepper (Safed Mirch)

White pepper is a black peppercorn with the skin removed. We use it a lot in our dishes in its ground form. It has a less intense taste than black pepper and cannot be seen in food due to its colour.

OTHER INGREDIENTS

Clarified Butter

Clarified butter, or ghee, is the fat that separates from the milk solids once butter is heated. Ghee is used in India as a cooking oil and is brushed on hot roti and naan.

Chicken

We use skinless thigh fillets in preference to breast in our recipes because we find that thighs are more succulent with our style of cooking. Chicken breasts will cook faster and dry out more than chicken thighs. We also find that chicken thighs take on the flavours of our marinades better.

Fish

We prefer to use gurnard or tarakihi for our dishes. Fish can be very soft and break apart, especially with our style of cooking. We find gurnard and tarakihi hold together and absorb our spice flavours well.

Jaggery

Jaggery is an unrefined sugar that comes from sugar cane juice. It is sold in a hard block and can be found at your local Indian supermarket.

Paneer

Paneer (see page 24) is a home-made Indian cheese that we make fresh at our restaurants and use in many of our vegetarian dishes.

Pastry Flour

We use pastry flour to make our samosas. We use this because once fried it is crisp on the outside but soft on the inside, which is what you want when breaking into your samosa. If you cannot find pastry flour at your local supermarket or Indian supermarket you can mix half standard flour and half high-grade flour for a similar result.

Tarka

A tarka is the base of a dish and usually consists of onion, ginger, garlic, tomato and spices. The tarka creates most of the flavour of the dish and the more time you spend cooking your tarka, the better your dish will be. Adding different spices, liquids and meats to your tarka can create many different dishes with a variety of textures and flavours.

PANEER

Paneer is a cheese that is used in many of our vegetarian dishes and some entrées. This recipe will produce more than enough for the dishes in this book. The extra paneer can be frozen and used later. You will need a muslin cloth to complete this recipe.

MAKES APPROXIMATELY 600 GRAMS

4 litres full fat milk

1 cup plain unsweetened yoghurt

½ cup lemon juice

Pour milk into a large saucepan over a high heat. Stir milk continuously to make sure it does not stick to bottom of pan. It will start to thicken. Continue cooking until milk comes to a boil, then turn heat down low. Add yoghurt and stir through for about a minute.

Add lemon juice. The milk will start to curdle and a layer of water will come to the surface (image 1). Cook for about another 2 minutes on a low heat so all the paneer comes together. Take off the heat and leave to cool for about 20 minutes.

Place muslin cloth over a strainer and pour cooled paneer and water over this (image 2). The muslin cloth will catch the paneer and the water will drain through. Wrap muslin cloth around paneer and tie ends tightly (image 3). Put wrapped paneer into a large mixing bowl. Place a small pot filled with water onto wrapped paneer to weigh it down (image 4). This will drain all the excess water out of the paneer. Leave to drain for 1 hour.

The paneer should now have cooled and be firm, and can be used for cooking. Any remaining paneer can go in the fridge and will last for 4 days. It can also be frozen.

1

2

3

4

ENTRÉES

ONION BHAJIS

If you like onion rings then you are sure to love our Onion Bhajis. This is a great snack to have any time of the day. In India, Onion Bhajis are usually served first with a cup of chai when guests arrive.

SERVES 6

- 2 onions, thinly sliced
- ½ tsp carom seeds
- ½ tsp cumin seeds
- ¾ tsp ground turmeric
- 1¼ tsp salt
- Pinch of red chilli powder
- Canola oil for deep frying
- 3 cups chickpea flour
- ½ cup water
- Chaat masala to garnish (optional)

Place sliced onions, carom and cumin seeds, turmeric, salt and chilli powder in a bowl and stir together.

Add oil to a large pan over a high heat so it is ready for frying when the batter is.

Working quickly, combine chickpea flour and water in a separate bowl to make the batter. Whisk until batter has a smooth custard-like consistency. Feel batter with your fingers and remove any small clumps of chickpea flour. Immediately add batter to onion and spices and stir together with your hands. Do not leave batter to sit as it will go watery and the onion bhajis will not come together correctly in the hot oil.

Make batter and onion mixture into a palm-sized fritter and carefully place in hot oil (the oil is ready when batter dropped in the oil rises to the surface). Repeat with remaining mixture. The bhajis can be a bit fiddly so it is best to fry one at a time. Fry onion bhajis until golden brown.

Garnish with chaat masala, if wished.

TANDOORI PRAWNS OR FISH

For seafood lovers Tandoori Prawns or Fish is a winner. The marinade used for this dish really lifts the taste of the seafood, further enhanced with Punjabi flavours. Marinate overnight for best results or for at least 4 hours. You will need 6 wooden skewers for this recipe.

SERVES 6

- **2 tbsp plain unsweetened yoghurt**
- **1 tbsp mustard oil**
- **¼ tsp ground white pepper**
- **1 tsp salt**
- **1½ tsp ground turmeric**
- **½ tsp carom seeds**
- **½ tsp ground fenugreek**
- **½ tsp crushed fresh ginger**
- **½ tsp crushed fresh garlic**
- **24 large prawn cutlets, deveined and shells removed; or 3 gurnard fillets, deboned and cut into 12 pieces**
- **Chaat masala to garnish**
- **Lemon or lime juice to season**

Soak wooden skewers in cold water a few hours ahead of time so they do not burn during cooking.

Place yoghurt, oil, white pepper, salt, spices, ginger and garlic in a bowl and mix together to form a smooth marinade. Gently mix prawns or fish through marinade and refrigerate for at least 4 hours.

Thread prawns or fish onto skewers and cook on a griddle plate or barbecue. Do not drench fish or prawns in marinade as they will not cook through fully. Cook on both sides until the fish or prawns are fully heated. Make sure you do not overcook fish or prawns – they should remain juicy.

Garnish with chaat masala and drizzle with lemon juice.

CHOOZA TIKKA AND BARRA KEBAB

Chooza Tikka and Barra Kebab are great to serve with drinks before a main meal. Traditionally cooked in the tandoor, this recipe has been adapted for you to cook at home. Marinate the meat overnight for best results or for at least 4 hours.

SERVES 6

- ½ tbsp canola oil
- 1 tsp paprika
- 1 quantity Tandoori Masala Marinade (see below)
- 500g boneless, skinless chicken thighs, cut into 12 even pieces; or 12 medium lamb chops
- 2 tbsp lemon juice
- Chaat masala to garnish
- Freshly chopped coriander and finely sliced red onion to garnish
- Lemon juice to season

Heat oil in a small pan over a low heat. Add paprika and mix through until the oil becomes a dark red colour. Make sure you do not burn the paprika. Once the oil has changed colour, remove from heat and strain the oil to separate it from the paprika grains. Leave oil to cool.

Mix chicken or lamb and lemon juice through Tandoori Masala Marinade. Add cooled paprika oil for colour. Place mixture in refrigerator for at least 4 hours to marinate.

Cook chicken or lamb on a medium hot griddle plate or barbecue. Do not drench meat in marinade as it will not cook through fully.

If cooking chicken, cook it for 5–7 minutes. To check if it is cooked, slice it in the middle and make sure the centre is not pink. (Alternatively, cook chicken in the oven. See Variation on page 42 for instructions.) If cooking lamb, cook it for a few minutes on each side. It should be medium for the best flavour. (To tell if the meat is medium, it should feel like the fleshy part under your thumb when you touch the tips of your thumb and ringfinger together.)

Garnish with chaat masala, freshly chopped coriander and red onion, and drizzle with lemon juice.

TANDOORI MASALA MARINADE

- 2 tbsp plain unsweetened yoghurt
- ½ tsp ground white pepper
- 1 tsp salt
- ½ tsp ground fenugreek
- 1 tsp garam masala
- 1 tsp crushed fresh garlic
- 1 tsp crushed fresh ginger

Tandoori Masala Marinade

To make marinade, combine yoghurt, white pepper, salt, spices, garlic and ginger in a bowl and mix together until a smooth marinade is reached.

PANEER ALOO TIKKI

Paneer Aloo Tikki are a delicious mix of potato, paneer, breadcrumbs and spices. They are sold by street vendors all over North India. If you are looking for an interesting vege patty for a burger, Paneer Aloo Tikki are a great option.

SERVES 6

- **2 medium Agria potatoes, peeled and boiled until tender**
- **100g paneer (see page 24)**
- **½ tsp crushed fresh ginger**
- **½ tsp salt**
- **1 green chilli, seeded and diced**
- **¼ tsp ground white pepper**
- **2½ tbsp fine breadcrumbs**
- **1½ tbsp chopped fresh coriander**
- **Canola oil for pan-frying**
- **Chaat masala to garnish**

Grate potatoes and paneer with a medium-sized grater. Place in a mixing bowl with ginger, salt, chilli and white pepper. Mix to combine.

Add breadcrumbs and 1 tablespoon coriander. Use your fingers to mix until combined.

Roll into balls slightly larger than a golf ball and flatten into patties.

Heat oil in a large frying pan over a medium heat and cook patties until golden brown (about 3 minutes on each side).

Garnish with chaat masala and remaining coriander.

PANEER TIKKA

Paneer Tikka is our most popular vegetarian starter from the tandoor. Large cubes of paneer, capsicums and red onion are all marinated in yoghurt and spices. When you are having a barbecue, Paneer Tikka is a great option for vegetarians. Marinate overnight for best results or for at least 4 hours. You will need 6 wooden skewers for this recipe.

SERVES 6

- 2 tbsp plain unsweetened yoghurt
- 1 tbsp mustard oil
- ¼ tsp ground white pepper
- 1 tsp salt
- 1½ tsp ground turmeric
- ½ tsp carom seeds
- ½ tsp ground fenugreek
- ½ tsp crushed fresh ginger
- ½ tsp crushed fresh garlic
- 600g paneer, cut into 4cm x 4cm cubes (see page 24)
- ½ green capsicum, cut into 4cm x 4cm cubes
- ½ red capsicum, cut into 4cm x 4cm cubes
- ½ red onion, cut into 4cm x 4cm cubes
- Chaat masala to garnish
- Lemon juice to season

Soak wooden skewers in cold water a few hours ahead of time so they do not burn during cooking.

Place yoghurt, oil, white pepper, salt, spices, ginger and garlic in a bowl and mix together to a smooth marinade. Gently mix cubed paneer, capsicum and onion through marinade. Marinate mixture in refrigerator for at least 4 hours.

Thread pieces of paneer, capsicum and onion onto skewers and cook on a medium hot griddle plate or barbecue. Do not drench paneer, capsicum and onion in marinade. Cook until paneer is fully heated through and it softens.

Garnish with chaat masala and drizzle with lemon juice.

Variation

An alternative way to cook Paneer Tikka is to preheat an oven to 220°C fan bake. Line a baking tray with baking paper and place marinated paneer cubes, capsicum and onion that have been threaded on skewers evenly on the baking paper. Do not cover paneer, capsicum or onion with any excess marinade or they will not cook through fully. Place the baking tray in the oven and cook for 10 minutes. The edges of the paneer will char – this is a good sign that the paneer is fully cooked.

VEGETABLE SAMOSAS

Making a good-looking and great-tasting samosa is an art. It may take a couple of attempts to get the shape right but once you do there is no looking back. Our Vegetable Samosas are one of our most popular starters and will surely be a hit at your dining table. Vegetable Samosas go perfectly with Tamarind Chutney (see page 146). The pastry should be made first and then placed in the refrigerator to cool while you make the samosa filling.

SERVES 6

SAMOSA PASTRY

- 1½ cups pastry flour (see page 23)
- 3 tbsp canola oil
- ¼ cup water
- ½ tsp carom seeds
- ½ tsp salt

SAMOSA FILLING

- 2 medium Agria potatoes, peeled and boiled until tender
- 3 tbsp canola oil
- ½ tsp cumin seeds
- ½ tsp coriander seeds
- 1 tsp crushed fresh ginger
- ¼ onion, finely chopped
- ½ cup green peas (frozen is fine)
- ½ tsp ground turmeric
- ½ tsp ground white pepper
- ½ tsp salt

Samosa Pastry

Put pastry flour in a large bowl with oil, water, carom seeds and salt. Knead mixture with your hands until well combined. Only add extra water if pastry is too dry – if pastry becomes too wet it will not fold together when adding filling.

Roll pastry into a 15cm-long roll and cut into three even pieces of 5cm each (image 1 on page 40). Roll each piece into a ball. Sprinkle some pastry flour on bench. Using a rolling pin, flatten each ball (image 2) and roll into three sheets about 22cm × 10cm (image 3). The sheets should be slightly thicker than paper thin. Add another sprinkle of pastry flour to each sheet. Place sheets on top of each other and cut in half (image 4).

Refrigerate pastry while you make the filling.

Samosa Filling

Mash potatoes to a chunky consistency and leave in a mixing bowl.

Heat oil in a pan over a low heat and add cumin and coriander seeds. Lightly toast. Add ginger and onion and fry until onion begins to brown. Mix through peas, turmeric, white pepper and salt until combined. Remove from heat. This mixture is called Samosa Tarka.

Evenly mix Samosa Tarka through potatoes.

Continued on page 40

To Assemble
1 quantity Samosa Pastry
Bowl of water
1 quantity Samosa Filling
Canola oil for deep-frying

Hold pastry sheet half in your hand with cut edge facing away from you. Dip finger into water bowl and lightly wet the entire straight edge. Fold top left of straight edge over to halfway point (image 5) then fold right edge onto this to make a cone shape. Flip pastry cone over so the tip of it is pointing to the floor (image 6).

With your other hand, roll filling into a tube shape that tapers down slightly at the tip to fit into point of cone. Stuff filling into cone

1

2

3

4

(image 7), leaving enough pastry to fold over and cover samosa base (image 8). Wet lip of samosa and fold over base, then fold over again.

Repeat with remaining pastry and filling.

Place oil in a large saucepan over a high heat. The oil is hot enough when you can drop a small piece of pastry into it and the pastry rises to the surface. Cook samosas until golden brown. It is best to cook as many samosas as you can at the same time, without crowding the saucepan. This means each samosa is cooked at the same temperature and you will get an even colour on all the samosas.

5

6

7

8

MALAI TIKKA

Malai Tikka is our mildest chicken starter. This is a nice way to introduce your friends and family to Indian cuisine because of its subtle flavours. Children love this dish when they come to our restaurants. Marinate overnight for best results or for at least 4 hours.

SERVES 6

- ¾ cup cream
- 2 tbsp crushed cashew nuts
- 50g Edam (or any mild cheese), grated
- 1 egg
- 1 tsp salt
- ¼ tsp ground white pepper
- 1 tsp green cardamom powder
- 1 tsp crushed fresh garlic
- 1 tsp crushed fresh ginger
- 500g skinless, boneless chicken thighs, cut into 12 pieces
- Chaat masala to garnish
- Freshly chopped coriander to garnish
- Lemon juice to season

In a bowl, mix together cream, cashews, cheese, egg, salt, white pepper, cardomom, garlic and ginger until a smooth marinade is reached. Gently mix chicken through marinade.

Place mixture in refrigerator for at least 4 hours to marinate.

Cook chicken on a medium hot griddle plate or barbecue for 5–7 minutes. Do not drench chicken in marinade as it will not cook through fully. To check if chicken is cooked, slice it in the middle and make sure the centre is not pink.

Remove chicken from the tray. Garnish with chaat masala and freshly chopped coriander and drizzle with lemon juice.

Variation

An alternative way to cook the chicken is to preheat an oven to 220°C fan bake. Line a baking tray with baking paper and place chicken thighs evenly on the baking paper. Do not cover chicken with any excess marinade or it will not cook through fully.

Place the baking tray in the oven and cook for 10 minutes. The edges of the chicken will char – this is a good sign that the chicken is fully cooked.

TANDOORI MUSHROOMS

Tandoori Mushrooms are traditionally cooked in the tandoor so we have modified this recipe for you to cook at home. The mushrooms are very juicy and full of flavour as they absorb the marinade very well. Marinate the mushrooms overnight for best results or for at least 4 hours. You will need 6 wooden skewers for this recipe.

SERVES 6

- ½ tbsp canola oil
- 1 tsp paprika
- 2 tbsp plain unsweetened yoghurt
- 1 tbsp cream
- ¼ tsp ground white pepper
- ½ tsp ground fenugreek
- ½ tsp salt
- ½ tsp garam masala
- ½ tsp crushed fresh garlic
- ½ tsp crushed fresh ginger
- 18 button mushrooms
- ½ tbsp lemon juice
- Chaat masala to garnish
- Lemon juice to season

Soak wooden skewers in cold water a few hours ahead of time so they do not burn during cooking.

Heat oil in a small pan over a low heat. Add paprika and mix through until the oil becomes a dark red colour. Make sure you do not burn the paprika. Once the oil has changed colour, remove from heat and strain the oil to separate it from the paprika grains. Leave oil to cool.

Place yoghurt, cream, white pepper, fenugreek, salt, garam masala, garlic, ginger and paprika oil in a bowl and mix thoroughly until a smooth consistency is reached.

Add mushrooms and stir to cover evenly with the marinade. Stir through lemon juice. Marinate for at least 4 hours.

Preheat oven to 200°C fan bake. Line a baking tray with baking paper.

Thread mushrooms on skewers and place on lined baking tray. Bake in oven for 10–15 minutes until cooked. Remove the mushrooms from the tray. Sprinkle with chaat masala and drizzle with extra lemon juice.

ACHAARI TIKKA

Out of all the tikka recipes in this book, the Achaari Tikka has the most depth in flavour because of the mix of spices that it is marinated in. If you enjoy spicier food you will really enjoy Achaari Tikka. Marinate overnight for best results or for at least 4 hours.

SERVES 6

- ½ tbsp onion seeds
- 1 tbsp mustard seeds
- 1½ tbsp fennel seeds
- ½ tbsp fenugreek seeds
- 2 tbsp plain unsweetened yoghurt
- 2 tbsp mustard oil
- 1 tsp salt
- ¼ tsp ground white pepper
- 1½ tsp ground turmeric
- 1 tsp crushed fresh garlic
- 1 tsp crushed fresh ginger
- 500g skinless, boneless chicken thighs, cut into 12 pieces
- 1 tbsp lemon juice
- Chaat masala to garnish
- Chopped fresh coriander to garnish
- Lemon juice to season

Place onion, mustard, fennel and fenugreek seeds in a spice grinder or mortar and pestle and grind to a powdered consistency.

In a bowl, mix together ground spices, yoghurt, oil, salt, white pepper, turmeric, garlic and ginger until a smooth marinade is reached.

Add chicken and lemon juice and gently mix through marinade.

Put mixture in refrigerator for at least 4 hours to marinate.

Cook chicken on a medium hot griddle plate or barbecue for 5–7 minutes. Do not drench in marinade as the chicken will not cook through fully. To check if chicken is cooked, slice it in the middle and make sure the centre is not pink.

Remove chicken from the tray. Sprinkle with chaat masala and chopped fresh coriander and drizzle with lemon juice.

Variation

An alternative way to cook the chicken is to preheat an oven to 220°C fan bake. Line a baking tray with baking paper and place chicken thighs evenly on the baking paper. Do not cover chicken with any excess marinade or it will not cook through fully.

Place the baking tray in the oven and cook for 10 minutes. The edges of the chicken will char – this is a good sign that the chicken is fully cooked.

CHICKEN MAINS

CHICKEN TIKKA MASALA

Chicken Tikka Masala is one of the most popular dishes at Little India. The founders of Little India, Sukhmohan and Joanna Gill, studied in England and at the time Chicken Tikka Masala was one of the most popular curries at all the English curry houses. They took the famous Chicken Tikka Masala of England, perfected the recipe, and made it their own. Note the chicken needs to be marinated in Tandoori Masala Marinade (see page 32) for at least 4 hours before you start making the dish.

SERVES 6

- ½ tbsp canola oil
- 1 tsp paprika
- ½ cup plain unsweetened yoghurt
- 500g skinless, boneless chicken thighs, marinated in Tandoori Masala Marinade (see page 32) for at least 4 hours
- 3 tbsp canola oil
- 1 onion, finely diced
- 1 tbsp crushed fresh garlic
- 1 tbsp crushed fresh ginger
- 1 tsp ground turmeric
- 1½ tsp garam masala
- 1 tsp salt
- 1 tsp ground fenugreek
- 2 medium tomatoes, diced
- 3 tbsp tomato paste
- 1 cup cream
- ½ cup boiling water
- Salt and red chilli powder to taste
- Cream to garnish
- Chopped fresh coriander to garnish (optional)

Add first measure of oil to a large pan over a medium heat. Add paprika and mix through until it releases its red colour. Remove from heat and leave to cool. Once cool, add to yoghurt and mix through. Set aside.

Preheat oven to 220°C fan bake. Line a baking tray with baking paper and place chicken thighs evenly on the baking paper. Do not cover chicken with excess marinade or it will not cook through fully.

Place the baking tray in the oven and cook for 10 minutes. The edges of the chicken will char – this is a good sign that the chicken is fully cooked. Cut cooked chicken into 3cm × 3cm cubes.

While chicken is cooking, heat second measure of oil in a pan and add onion, stirring continuously so it doesn't stick to bottom of pan. Cook until almost brown. Stir in garlic and ginger and cook until softened and browned. Add turmeric, garam masala, salt and fenugreek and continue cooking until you can start to smell the spice aromas.

Stir through tomato and tomato paste and keep cooking until you start to see oil separating from onion and spice mixture. Be sure to take your time with this. The mix that you are making is called a Tarka.

Add cubed chicken to Tarka and cook until the chicken is fully heated through (about 5 minutes). Once this is done turn heat down low and stir through yoghurt mix and cream. Slowly increase heat so yoghurt and cream do not curdle. Carefully pour in boiling water and cook until water, yoghurt and cream come together and sauce begins to bubble.

Season to taste with salt and chilli powder. Garnish with a swirl of cream and freshly chopped coriander if wished.

BHUNA CHICKEN

Bhuna Chicken is one of our drier dishes and has beautiful crisp, fresh flavours. The cooking style is almost like making a stir-fry. Bhuna means to cook over a high heat while stirring your ingredients to prevent them burning and sticking to the pan. Note the chicken needs to be marinated in Tandoori Masala Marinade (see page 32) for at least 4 hours before you start making the dish.

SERVES 6

- 500g skinless, boneless chicken thighs, marinated in Tandoori Masala Marinade (see page 32) for at least 4 hours
- ¼ cup canola oil
- 2 tbsp crushed fresh ginger
- 2 tbsp crushed fresh garlic
- 1 tsp ground turmeric
- 1½ tsp garam masala
- 1 tsp salt
- 1 medium tomato, diced
- 2 tbsp tomato paste
- 2 onions, thinly sliced
- 1 green capsicum, cut julienne style
- ½ cup chopped fresh coriander
- Salt and red chilli powder to taste
- Sliced red onion or chopped fresh coriander to garnish

Preheat oven to 220°C fan bake. Line a baking tray with baking paper and place chicken thighs evenly on the baking paper. Do not cover chicken with excess marinade or it will not cook through fully.

Place the baking tray in the oven and cook for 10 minutes. The edges of the chicken will char – this is a good sign that the chicken is fully cooked. Cut cooked chicken into 5cm × 0.5cm slices.

While chicken is cooking, heat oil in a large pan over a medium heat and add ginger and garlic. Add turmeric, garam masala and salt and increase heat to high. Mix together thoroughly, making sure you do not burn ginger and garlic and mixture does not stick to the pan.

When you can smell the spice aromas coming through, it is time to add the sliced chicken, tomato and tomato paste. Cook until chicken is heated through (about 5 minutes). Stir through onion, capsicum and coriander. Continue to stir-fry until capsicum starts to soften.

Season with salt and chilli powder to taste. Garnish with sliced red onion or freshly chopped coriander.

CHICKEN KORMA

Chicken Korma is traditionally a mild dish made with a creamy sauce and almond paste. It is a perfect dish for first-time curry eaters. Note the chicken needs to be marinated in Tandoori Masala Marinade (see page 32) for at least 4 hours before you start making the dish.

SERVES 6

- 2 tbsp slivered almonds
- 1 tbsp whole cashew nuts
- 500g skinless, boneless chicken thighs, marinated in Tandoori Masala Marinade (see page 32) for at least 4 hours
- 3 tbsp canola oil
- 1 onion, puréed to a fine consistency
- 1 tbsp crushed fresh garlic
- 1 tbsp crushed fresh ginger
- 1 tsp ground turmeric
- 1½ tsp garam masala
- 1 tsp salt
- 1 tsp ground fenugreek
- 2 medium tomatoes, diced
- 3 tbsp tomato paste
- 1 cup cream
- ½ cup milk
- ½ cup boiling water
- Salt and red chilli powder to taste
- Slivered almonds or chopped fresh coriander to garnish

Soak almonds and cashews in water for at least 30 minutes. Strain and pat dry. Blend almonds and cashews together using either a handheld blender or food processor until they form a smooth paste.

Preheat oven to 220°C fan bake. Line a baking tray with baking paper and place chicken thighs evenly on the baking paper. Do not cover chicken with excess marinade or it will not cook through fully.

Place the baking tray in the oven and cook for 10 minutes. The edges of the chicken will char – this is a good sign that the chicken is fully cooked. Slice cooked chicken into 5cm × 0.5cm pieces.

While chicken is cooking, heat oil in a large pan over a medium heat and add onion, stirring continuously so it doesn't stick to bottom of pan. Cook until almost brown.

Add garlic and ginger and cook until softened and browned. Mix in turmeric, garam masala, salt and fenugreek and continue cooking until you start to smell the spice aromas.

Stir through tomato and tomato paste and cook until you start to see oil separating from onion and spice mixture. Be sure to take your time with this and keep stirring so that it does not stick to bottom of pan. The mix that you are making is called a Tarka.

Add nut paste and sliced chicken to Tarka and cook until chicken is fully heated through (about 5 minutes). Turn heat down low and stir through cream and milk. Slowly increase heat so you do not curdle cream and milk.

Carefully pour in boiling water and cook until water and cream come together and sauce begins to bubble.

Season to taste with salt and chilli powder. Garnish with slivered almonds or chopped fresh coriander.

KADAI CHICKEN

Kadai Chicken is a mouth-watering dish with great depth of flavour. The tomatoes, onion, fresh coriander and cream create a thick gravy. This dish goes really well with our Lacha Parantha (see page 134). Note the chicken needs to be marinated in Tandoori Masala Marinade (see page 32) for at least 4 hours before you start making the dish.

SERVES 6

- 500g skinless, boneless chicken thighs, marinated in Tandoori Masala Marinade (see page 32) for at least 4 hours
- 3 tbsp canola oil
- 2 tsp cumin seeds
- 1 onion, puréed to a fine consistency
- 1 tbsp crushed fresh garlic
- 1 tbsp crushed fresh ginger
- 1 tsp ground turmeric
- 1½ tsp garam masala
- 1 tsp salt
- 1 tbsp ground fenugreek
- 1 onion, thinly sliced
- 2 tomatoes, diced
- 3 tbsp tomato paste
- ½ cup chopped fresh coriander
- 1 cup cream
- ½ cup boiling water
- Salt and red chilli powder to taste
- Chopped fresh coriander to garnish

Preheat oven to 220°C fan bake. Line a baking tray with baking paper and place chicken thighs evenly on the baking paper. Do not cover chicken with excess marinade or it will not cook through fully.

Place the baking tray in the oven and cook for 10 minutes. The edges of the chicken will char – this is a good sign that the chicken is fully cooked. Cut cooked chicken into 5cm × 0.5cm slices.

While chicken is cooking, heat oil in a large pan over a low heat. Add cumin seeds and cook until you start to smell the aroma of the cumin seeds coming through. Add puréed onion, stirring continuously so it doesn't stick to bottom of pan. Cook until almost brown.

Add garlic and ginger and cook until softened and browned. Mix in turmeric, garam masala, salt and fenugreek and continue cooking until you start to smell the spice aromas.

Add thinly sliced onion and fry until it begins to soften.

Stir through tomato and tomato paste and keep cooking until you start to see oil separating from onion and spice mixture. Be sure to take your time with this and keep stirring so that it does not stick to bottom of pan. The mix that you are making is called a Tarka.

Add sliced chicken and coriander to Tarka and cook until chicken is fully heated through (about 5 minutes). Once this is done turn heat down low and stir through cream. Slowly increase heat so cream does not curdle.

Carefully pour in boiling water and cook until water and cream come together and sauce begins to bubble.

Season to taste with salt and chilli powder. Garnish with chopped fresh coriander.

BUTTER CHICKEN

There is a common misconception that Butter Chicken does not exist in India. This is not true. In India it is more commonly known as Murg Makhani (Chicken Buttery) or, as we call it at Little India, Murg Mumtaz. Sadly, however, in New Zealand the taste of Butter Chicken has been Westernised as the majority of places that sell it add a lot of sugar to the recipe. This is certainly not the case at Little India. Note the chicken needs to be marinated in Tandoori Masala Marinade (see page 32) for at least 4 hours before you start making the dish.

SERVES 6

- 500g skinless, boneless chicken thighs, marinated in Tandoori Masala Marinade (see page 32) for at least 4 hours
- 3 tbsp canola oil
- 1 onion, puréed to a fine consistency
- 1 tbsp crushed fresh garlic
- 1 tbsp crushed fresh ginger
- 1 tsp ground turmeric
- 1½ tsp garam masala
- 1 tsp salt
- 1 tbsp ground fenugreek
- 2 medium tomatoes, diced
- 3 tbsp tomato paste
- 1½ cups cream
- 2 tbsp finely crushed cashew nuts
- ½ cup boiling water
- Salt and red chilli powder to taste
- Finely crushed cashew nuts or chopped fresh coriander to garnish

Preheat oven to 220°C fan bake. Line a baking tray with baking paper and place chicken thighs evenly on the baking paper. Do not cover chicken with excess marinade or it will not cook through fully.

Place the baking tray in the oven and cook for 10 minutes. The edges of the chicken will char – this is a good sign that the chicken is fully cooked. Cut chicken into 3cm × 3cm cubes.

While chicken is cooking, heat oil in a large pan over a medium heat and add onion, stirring continuously so it doesn't stick to bottom of pan. Cook until almost brown.

Add garlic and ginger and cook until softened and brown. Add turmeric, garam masala, salt and fenugreek and continue cooking until you start to smell the spice aromas.

Stir through tomato and tomato paste and keep cooking until you start to see oil separating from onion and spice mixture. Be sure to take your time with this and keep stirring so that it does not stick to bottom of pan. The mix that you are making is called a Tarka.

Add cubed chicken to Tarka and cook until chicken is fully heated through (about 5 minutes). Once this is done, turn heat down low and stir through cream. Slowly increase heat so cream does not curdle. Mix through cashew nuts.

Carefully pour in boiling water and cook until water and cream come together and sauce begins to bubble.

Season to taste with salt and chilli powder. Garnish with crushed cashew nuts or chopped fresh coriander.

CHICKEN BIRYANI

Biryani comes from Hyderabad and is a complete meal in itself. The cumin, cardamom, cloves and cinnamon are used in their whole form to give a wonderful depth of flavour and fragrance. Note the chicken needs to be marinated in Tandoori Masala Marinade (see page 32) for at least 4 hours before you start making the dish.

SERVES 6

- 500g skinless, boneless chicken thighs, marinated in Tandoori Masala Marinade (see page 32) for at least 4 hours
- 3 tbsp canola oil
- 1 tsp cumin seeds
- 4 green cardamom pods
- 4 cloves
- 1 stick cinnamon (about 5cm long)
- 1 onion, puréed to a fine consistency
- 1 tbsp each crushed garlic and ginger
- 1 tsp ground turmeric
- 1½ tsp garam masala
- 1 tsp salt
- 1 tbsp ground fenugreek
- 2 medium tomatoes, diced
- 2 tbsp tomato paste
- ½ cup chopped fresh coriander
- ½ cup frozen green peas
- 1 cup cream
- 1 quantity Basmati Rice (see page 114)
- Salt and red chilli powder to taste
- Chopped fresh coriander to garnish

Preheat oven to 220°C fan bake. Line a baking tray with baking paper and place chicken thighs evenly on the baking paper. Do not cover chicken with excess marinade or it will not cook through.

Place the baking tray in the oven and cook for 10 minutes. The edges of the chicken will char – this is a good sign that the chicken is fully cooked. Cut cooked chicken into 5cm × 0.5cm slices.

While the chicken is cooking, heat oil in a large pan over a low heat and add cumin seeds, cardamom, cloves and cinnamon. Cook until you start to smell the aromas of the spices coming through.

Add onion, stirring continuously so it doesn't stick to bottom of pan. Cook until almost brown.

Stir in garlic and ginger and cook until softened and browned. Add turmeric, garam masala, salt and fenugreek and continue cooking until you start to smell the spice aromas.

Stir through tomato and tomato paste and keep cooking until you start to see oil separating from onion and spice mixture. Be sure to take your time with this and keep stirring so that it does not stick to bottom of pan. The mix that you are making is called a Tarka.

Add sliced chicken and coriander and cook until chicken is fully heated through (about 5 minutes). Add peas and mix through. Turn heat down low and stir through cream. Slowly increase heat so that cream does not curdle.

Mix cooked rice through chicken mixture. The rice needs to combine with chicken mixture and should turn into the colour of the mix. Cook until rice is fully heated. Season to taste with salt and chilli powder.

Garnish with chopped fresh coriander if wished.

CHICKEN VINDALOO

Vindaloo is a Goan dish with Portuguese influence. It is cooked with vinegar and capsicum to give it its unique flavour. Vindaloo is traditionally a hot dish and goes well with Naan bread (see page 130). Note the chicken needs to be marinated in Tandoori Masala Marinade (see page 32) for at least 4 hours before you start making the dish.

SERVES 6

VINDALOO PASTE

- 1 tsp whole black peppercorns
- 4 cloves
- 2 tsp fennel seeds
- 1 tsp fenugreek seeds
- 6 dried red chillies
- 3 fresh green chillies
- 2 tsp each crushed garlic and ginger
- ¼ cup canola oil
- 1 tbsp vinegar

CURRY

- 500g skinless, boneless chicken thighs, marinated in Tandoori Masala Marinade (see page 32) for at least 4 hours
- 1 onion, finely diced
- 1 tbsp each crushed garlic and ginger
- 1 tsp ground turmeric
- 1½ tsp garam masala
- 2 medium tomatoes, diced
- 2 tbsp tomato paste
- 1½ tbsp Vindaloo Paste
- ½ green capsicum, cut julienne style
- Chopped fresh coriander or finely sliced green capsicum to garnish

In a spice grinder (or using a mortar and pestle), grind peppercorns, cloves, fennel and fenugreek seeds, dried red chillies and half a teaspoon of salt into a fine powder and set aside for later use. Grind green chillies, garlic, ginger, oil and vinegar into a fine paste. Mix spice powder and chilli paste together to make your Vindaloo Paste.

Preheat oven to 220°C fan bake. Line a baking tray with baking paper and place chicken thighs evenly on the baking paper. Do not cover chicken with excess marinade or it will not cook through fully.

Place the baking tray in the oven and cook for 10 minutes. The edges of the chicken will char – this is a good sign that the chicken is fully cooked. Slice chicken into 5cm × 0.5cm pieces.

While chicken is cooking, heat 3 tablespoons of canola oil in a large pan over a medium heat and add onion, stirring continuously. Cook until almost brown. Add garlic and ginger and cook until it softens and browns. Add turmeric, garam masala and 1 teaspoon salt and continue cooking until you start to smell the spice aromas.

Stir through tomato and tomato paste and keep cooking until you start to see oil separating from onion and spice mixture. Be sure to take your time with this. The mixture you are making is called a Tarka.

Mix Vindaloo Paste through the Tarka until fully combined. Add sliced chicken and capsicum and continue cooking until chicken is fully heated through (about 5 minutes).

Pour in 2 cups cold water and cook until everything has combined into a sauce and it begins to bubble. Turn heat down and simmer until you see some oil coming to the surface of the dish.

Season to taste with salt and red chilli powder. Garnish with chopped fresh coriander or finely sliced capsicum.

LAMB MAINS

LAMB BHUNA GOSHT

Lamb Bhuna Gosht is one of our drier lamb curries. Slow and steady cooking of this dish develops a beautiful depth of flavour. Poppadoms go very well with this dish.

SERVES 6

- **¼ cup canola oil**
- **1 onion, puréed to a fine consistency**
- **2 tbsp crushed fresh garlic**
- **2 tbsp crushed fresh ginger**
- **500g lean lamb leg, cut into 3cm x 3cm cubes**
- **1 tsp ground turmeric**
- **1½ tsp garam masala**
- **1 tsp salt**
- **1 tsp paprika**
- **3 medium tomatoes, diced**
- **½ cup tomato purée**
- **½ cup chopped fresh coriander**
- **1 cup cold water**
- **Salt and red chilli powder to taste**
- **Chopped fresh coriander to garnish**

Heat oil in a large pan over a low heat. Add puréed onion, stirring continuously so it doesn't stick to bottom of pan. Cook until almost brown.

Add garlic and ginger and cook until softened and browned.

Add cubed lamb and cook until just browned. Add turmeric, garam masala, salt and paprika and continue cooking until you start to smell the spice aromas.

Stir through tomato and keep cooking until you start to see oil separating from onion and spice mixture. Be sure to take your time with this and keep stirring so that it does not stick to bottom of pan.

Add tomato purée, coriander and cold water and cook until these combine. Put a lid on the pan and continue to simmer over a low heat until oil has separated from gravy. This can take a few hours and you may need to add more water if the gravy dries out too much. Remember this is a drier dish so use extra water only if needed. Once lamb is tender the dish is done.

Season to taste with salt and chilli powder. Garnish with chopped fresh coriander.

Cook's Note

Lamb dishes take a long time to cook. You will need to be patient and cook the lamb until tender, which can take 2 hours or more. You can use a pressure cooker to speed up the process.

LAMB MADRAS

Lamb Madras is a spicy dish rich in ginger and fenugreek flavours. Our madras is a favourite with our staff on a cold winter's day as it warms the heart and soul with its intense flavours.

SERVES 6

- ¼ cup canola oil
- 1 onion, puréed to a fine consistency
- 1 tbsp crushed fresh garlic
- 2 tbsp crushed fresh ginger
- 500g lean lamb leg, cut into 3cm x 3cm cubes
- 1 tsp ground turmeric
- 1½ tsp garam masala
- 1 tsp salt
- 1 tsp paprika
- 1 tbsp ground fenugreek
- 1 tbsp finely diced green chilli
- 2 medium tomatoes, diced
- ½ cup tomato purée
- ½ cup chopped fresh coriander
- 2 cups cold water
- Salt and red chilli powder to taste
- Chopped fresh coriander or finely sliced ginger to garnish

Heat oil in a large pan over a low heat. Add onion, stirring continuously so it doesn't stick to bottom of pan. Cook until almost brown.

Stir in garlic and ginger and cook until softened and browned.

Add cubed lamb and cook until just browned. Add turmeric, garam masala, salt, paprika, fenugreek and green chilli and continue cooking until you start to smell the spice aromas.

Stir through tomato and keep cooking until you start to see oil separating from onion and spice mixture. Be sure to take your time with this and keep stirring so that it does not stick to bottom of pan.

Add tomato purée, coriander and water and cook until these combine.

Put a lid on the pan and continue to simmer over a low heat until oil has separated from sauce and comes to the surface. This can take a few hours and you may need to add more water if sauce reduces too much. Once oil has separated and lamb is tender, the dish is done.

Season to taste with salt and chilli powder. Garnish with chopped fresh coriander or finely sliced ginger.

Cook's Note

Lamb dishes take a long time to cook. You will need to be patient and cook the lamb until tender, which can take 2 hours or more. You can use a pressure cooker to speed up the process.

LAMB SAAGWALA

Lamb Saagwala, also known as Lamb Saag, is a dish for spinach lovers. The puréed spinach adds a light consistency to the sauce and makes the dish green in colour. Lamb Saag is a great source of iron and a good way to get your kids eating spinach.

SERVES 6

- 3 bunches spinach, chopped
- ¼ cup canola oil
- 1 onion, diced
- 1 tbsp crushed fresh garlic
- 1 tbsp crushed fresh ginger
- 500g lean lamb leg, cut into 3cm x 3cm cubes
- 1 tsp ground turmeric
- 1½ tsp garam masala
- 1 tsp salt
- 1 tsp paprika
- 2 medium tomatoes, diced
- ½ cup tomato purée
- ½ cup chopped fresh coriander
- 2 cups cold water
- Salt and red chilli powder to taste
- Sliced tomato or chopped fresh coriander to garnish

Place spinach in a large pot and fill with water to just cover spinach. Simmer just until spinach softens (about 10 minutes). It is important not to cook this for too long. Strain water from softened spinach. Put spinach in a blender and process to a smooth paste.

Heat oil in a large pan over a low heat. Add onion, stirring continuously so that it doesn't stick to bottom of pan. Cook until almost brown. Stir in garlic and ginger and cook until softened and browned.

Add cubed lamb and cook until just browned. Add turmeric, garam masala, salt and paprika and continue cooking until you start to smell the spice aromas.

Stir through tomato and keep cooking until you start to see oil separating from onion and spice mixture. Be sure to take your time with this and keep stirring so that it does not stick to bottom of pan.

Add tomato purée, coriander and water and cook until this combines.

Put a lid on the pan and continue to simmer over a low heat until oil has separated from sauce and comes to the surface. It can take a few hours for the lamb to soften. You may also have to add some more water if sauce reduces too much. Once oil has separated and lamb is tender, add spinach paste and cook through (about 7 minutes). Add a little more water if required.

Season to taste with salt and chilli powder. Garnish with sliced tomato or fresh coriander.

Cook's Note

Lamb dishes take a long time to cook. You will need to be patient and cook the lamb until tender, which can take 2 hours or more. You can use a pressure cooker to speed up the process.

LAMB BIRYANI

Biryani comes from Hyderabad and is a complete meal in itself. Once you have perfected your biryani, it will have the wow factor and is a great way to impress your dinner guests.

SERVES 6

- ¼ cup canola oil
- 6 green cardamom pods
- 6 cloves
- 1 stick cinnamon (about 5cm long)
- 1 onion, puréed to a fine consistency
- 1 tbsp crushed fresh garlic
- 1 tbsp crushed fresh ginger
- 500g lean lamb leg, cut into 3cm x 3cm cubes
- 1 tsp ground turmeric
- 1½ tsp garam masala
- 1 tsp salt
- 1 tsp paprika
- 3 medium tomatoes, diced
- ½ cup tomato purée
- ½ cup chopped fresh coriander
- 2 cups cold water
- ½ cup cream
- Salt and red chilli powder to taste
- 1 quantity Basmati Rice (see page 114)
- Chopped fresh coriander to garnish (optional)

Heat oil in a large pan over a low heat and add cardamom, cloves and cinnamon. Cook until you start to smell the spice aromas coming through.

Add onion, stirring continuously so it doesn't stick to bottom of pan. Cook until almost brown. Stir in garlic and ginger and cook until softened and browned.

Add cubed lamb and cook until brown. Mix in turmeric, garam masala, salt and paprika and continue cooking until you start to smell the spice aromas.

Stir through tomato and keep cooking until you start to see oil separating from onion and spice mixture. Be sure to take your time with this and keep stirring so that it does not stick to bottom of pan.

Add tomato purée, coriander and cold water and cook until combined.

Place a lid on the pan and simmer over a low heat until oil has separated from sauce and comes to surface. It can take a few hours for the lamb to soften. You may have to add some more water if sauce reduces too much. Once oil has separated and lamb is tender, add cream and cook for 5 minutes.

Add cooked rice. The rice needs to combine with the lamb mixture and should turn into the colour of the mix. Cook until rice is fully heated.

Season to taste with salt and chilli powder.

Garnish with chopped fresh coriander if wished.

Cook's Note

Lamb dishes take a long time to cook. You will need to be patient and cook the lamb until tender, which can take 2 hours or more. You can use a pressure cooker to speed up the process.

ROGAN JOSH

Lamb Rogan Josh is a great go-to curry for first-time lamb curry cooks. Rogan is the oil that rises to the surface of the dish when cooked correctly.

SERVES 6

- ¼ cup canola oil
- 6 green cardamom pods
- 6 cloves
- 1 onion, puréed to a fine consistency
- 1 tbsp crushed fresh garlic
- 1 tbsp crushed fresh ginger
- 500g lean lamb leg, cut into 3cm x 3cm cubes
- 1 tsp ground turmeric
- 1½ tsp garam masala
- 1 tsp salt
- 1 tsp paprika
- 3 medium tomatoes, diced
- ½ cup tomato purée
- ½ cup chopped fresh coriander
- 2 cups cold water
- ¼ cup plain unsweetened yoghurt
- Salt and red chilli powder to taste
- Chopped fresh coriander to garnish (optional)

Heat oil in a large pan over a low heat. Add cardamom and cloves. Cook over a low heat until you start to smell the spice aromas coming through. Add onion, stirring continuously so it doesn't stick to bottom of pan. Cook until almost brown.

Stir in garlic and ginger and cook until softened and browned.

Add cubed lamb and cook until just browned. Add turmeric, garam masala, salt and paprika and continue cooking until you start to smell the spice aromas.

Stir through tomato and keep cooking until you start to see oil separating from onion and spice mixture. Be sure to take your time with this and keep stirring so that it does not stick to bottom of pan.

Add tomato purée, coriander and water and cook until this combines. Turn heat down low and stir through yoghurt. Slowly increase heat so that yoghurt does not curdle.

Put a lid on the pan and continue to simmer over a low heat until oil has separated from sauce and comes to surface. This can take a few hours. You may have to add some more water if sauce reduces too much. Once oil has separated and lamb is tender, the dish is done.

Season to taste with salt and chilli powder. Garnish with chopped fresh coriander, if wished.

Cook's Note

Lamb dishes take a long time to cook. You will need to be patient and cook the lamb until tender, which can take 2 hours or more. You can use a pressure cooker to speed up the process.

ACHAARI LAMB

Achaar is an Indian pickle which has heady, intense flavours. Indian pickles are used as a side to enhance the flavour of milder dishes. This dish has strong flavours and packs a punch. Because of its intense flavours, Achaari Lamb goes well with plain Basmati Rice or Roti (see pages 114 and 124).

SERVES 6

ACHAARI PASTE

- 1 tsp onion seeds
- 1 tsp mustard seeds
- 1 tsp fenugreek seeds
- 1 tbsp fennel seeds
- 1 tbsp mustard oil

- 3 tbsp mixed vegetable pickle
- ¼ cup canola oil
- 1 onion, finely diced
- 1 tbsp crushed fresh garlic
- 1 tbsp crushed fresh ginger
- 500g lean lamb leg, cut into 3cm x 3cm cubes
- 1 tsp ground turmeric
- 1½ tsp garam masala
- 1 tsp salt
- 1 tsp paprika
- 2 medium tomatoes, diced
- ½ cup tomato purée
- ½ cup chopped fresh coriander
- 2 cups cold water
- 1 tomato, cut into large chunks
- Salt and red chilli powder to taste
- Chopped fresh coriander to garnish

In a spice grinder, very finely grind onion, mustard, fenugreek and fennel seeds. Put ground spice mixture in a bowl and stir in mustard oil. This is your Achaari Paste. Set aside for later use.

Purée mixed vegetable pickle in a bowl and set aside.

Heat canola oil in a large pan over a low heat. Add onion, stirring continuously so it doesn't stick to bottom of pan. Cook until almost brown. Stir in garlic and ginger and cook until softened and browned.

Add cubed lamb and cook until just browned. Add turmeric, garam masala, salt and paprika and cook until you start to smell the spice aromas.

Stir through tomato and keep cooking until you start to see oil separating from onion and spice mixture. Be sure to take your time with this and keep stirring so that it does not stick to bottom of pan.

Add tomato purée, coriander, Achaari Paste and puréed pickle and stir through. Pour in water and mix through until everything combines.

Put a lid on the pan and continue to simmer over a low heat until oil has separated from sauce and comes to surface. It can take a few hours for the lamb to soften. You may have to add some more water if the sauce reduces too much. Once oil has separated and lamb is tender, add tomato chunks and cook through until they soften (about 5 minutes). Add a little more water if required.

Season to taste with salt and chilli powder. Garnish with chopped fresh coriander.

Cook's Note

Lamb dishes take a long time to cook. You will need to be patient and cook the lamb until tender, which can take 2 hours or more. You can use a pressure cooker to speed up the process.

LAMB DHANSAK

Lamb Dhansak is a Parsi dish. It is a complete meal containing protein, vegetables and pulses all in one.

SERVES 6

- ¼ cup yellow split peas
- 2 cups water
- 100g pumpkin, cut into chunks
- ½ carrot, sliced into rounds
- ½ courgette, sliced into rounds
- 8 green beans, sliced into 2cm pieces
- 4 small florets cauliflower
- ¼ cup canola oil
- ½ tsp coriander seeds
- 1 onion, puréed to a fine consistency
- 1 tbsp crushed fresh garlic
- 1 tbsp crushed fresh ginger
- 500g lean lamb leg, cut into 3cm x 3cm cubes
- 1 tsp ground turmeric
- 1½ tsp garam masala
- 1 tsp salt
- 1 tsp dhansak masala (see page 21)
- 1 tsp paprika
- 2 medium tomatoes, diced
- ½ cup tomato purée
- ½ cup chopped fresh coriander
- Salt and red chilli powder to taste
- Chopped fresh coriander to garnish

Put split peas in a bowl and add water to just cover split peas. With your hands, mix split peas through water. The water will go cloudy. Strain water from split peas and repeat until water is clear when you mix it. Once water is clear, cover bowl and leave split peas to soak for at least 1 hour. Remove cover and strain. Place split peas in a pot with 2 cups water. Bring to the boil for about 20 minutes, until you can squash split peas between your fingers. Strain and set aside.

Place pumpkin in a pot, cover with water and boil until soft.

Put carrot, courgette, green beans and cauliflower in a pot and boil until al dente. Strain and reserve pumpkin and vegetables.

Heat oil in a large pan over a low heat. Add coriander seeds and cook until you start to smell the spice aromas. Add onion, stirring continuously so it doesn't stick to bottom of pan. Cook until almost brown. Stir in garlic and ginger and cook until softened and browned. Add lamb and cook until just browned. Add turmeric, garam masala, salt, dhansak masala and paprika and cook until you smell the spices.

Stir through tomato and keep cooking until you start to see oil separating from onion and spice mixture. Be sure to take your time with this and keep stirring so that it does not stick to bottom of pan.

Add tomato purée, coriander, pumpkin, split peas and vegetables to lamb mix and simmer with a lid on. This can take a few hours. Once lamb is tender the dish is done. You may need to add more water if sauce reduces too much.

Season to taste with salt and chilli powder. Garnish with chopped fresh coriander.

Cook's Note

Lamb dishes take a long time to cook. You will need to be patient and cook the lamb until tender, which can take 2 hours or more. You can use a pressure cooker to speed up the process.

little India.

FISH AND PRAWN MAINS

PRAWN OR FISH MALABARI

Malabari is a dish from Mumbai. It is cooked with coconut, capsicum and cream, which gives the dish a beautiful rich sauce.

SERVES 6

- 3 tbsp canola oil
- 1 tsp carom seeds
- 1 onion, puréed to a fine consistency
- 1 tbsp crushed fresh garlic
- 1 tbsp crushed fresh ginger
- 1 tsp ground turmeric
- 1½ tsp garam masala
- 1 tsp salt
- 2 medium tomatoes, diced
- 3 tbsp tomato paste
- 24 large prawn cutlets, deveined and shells removed; or 500g gurnard fillets, deboned and cut into large chunks
- ½ onion, thinly sliced
- 1 green capsicum, cut julienne style
- 1 tbsp vinegar
- 3 tbsp desiccated coconut
- 1½ cups cream
- ½ cup boiling water
- Salt and red chilli powder to taste
- Chopped fresh coriander or finely sliced green capsicum and desiccated coconut to garnish

Heat oil in a large pan over a low heat and add carom seeds. Cook over a low heat until you start to smell the aroma of the carom seeds coming through. Add puréed onion, stirring continuously so it doesn't stick to bottom of pan. Cook until almost brown.

Stir in garlic and ginger and cook until softened and browned. Add turmeric, garam masala and salt and continue cooking until you start to smell the spice aromas.

Stir through tomato and tomato paste and keep cooking until you start to see oil separating from onion and spice mixture. Be sure to take your time with this and keep stirring so that it does not stick to bottom of pan. The mix that you are making is called a Tarka.

Add prawn cutlets or gurnard fillets, thinly sliced onion, capsicum, vinegar and desiccated coconut and stir through the Tarka. Turn heat down low and stir through cream. Slowly increase heat so that cream does not curdle.

Carefully pour in boiling water and cook until cream and water come together and sauce begins to bubble and thicken.

Season to taste with salt and chilli powder. Garnish with chopped fresh coriander or finely sliced capsicum and desiccated coconut.

PRAWN JHALFREZEE

Jhalfrezee is a dish that was created during the days of the Raj. 'Jhal' means hot and 'frezee' means stir-fried. This dish is cooked with coconut milk, red capsicum and spring onion.

SERVES 6

- 3 tbsp canola oil
- 6 cloves
- 2 sticks cinnamon (about 5cm long)
- 1 tsp carom seeds
- 1 tsp ground coriander
- 1 onion, finely diced
- 1 tbsp crushed fresh garlic
- 1 tbsp crushed fresh ginger
- 1 tsp ground turmeric
- 1½ tsp garam masala
- 1 tsp salt
- 2 medium tomatoes, diced
- 2 tbsp tomato paste
- 24 large prawn cutlets, deveined and shells removed
- 1 bunch spring onions, chopped
- 1 red capsicum, cut julienne style
- ½ cup coconut milk
- Salt and red chilli powder to taste
- Chopped spring onion or fresh coriander to garnish

6/1/14.

Heat oil in a large pan over a low heat and add cloves, cinnamon sticks, carom seeds and ground coriander. Cook until you start to smell the aromas of the spices coming through.

Add onion, stirring continuously so it doesn't stick to bottom of pan. Cook until almost brown.

Stir in garlic and ginger and cook until softened and browned. Add turmeric, garam masala and salt and continue cooking until you start to smell the spice aromas.

Stir through tomato and tomato paste and keep cooking until you start to see oil separating from onion and spice mixture. Be sure to take your time with this and keep stirring so that it does not stick to bottom of pan. The mix that you are making is called a Tarka.

Add prawn cutlets, spring onion and capsicum and stir through the Tarka. Turn heat down low and stir through coconut milk. Cook for 7–10 minutes until the prawns are cooked but still juicy.

Season to taste with salt and chilli powder. Garnish with chopped spring onion or fresh coriander.

PRAWN BIRYANI

In our Prawn Biryani, the cardomom, cloves and cinnamon are used in their whole form to give a wonderful depth of flavour and fragrance. This is a very popular dish in our restaurants.

SERVES 6

- **3 tbsp canola oil**
- **1 tsp carom seeds**
- **4 green cardamom pods**
- **4 cloves**
- **1 stick cinnamon (about 5cm long)**
- **1 onion, puréed to a fine consistency**
- **1 tbsp crushed fresh garlic**
- **1 tbsp crushed fresh ginger**
- **1 tsp ground turmeric**
- **1½ tsp garam masala**
- **1 tsp salt**
- **1 tbsp ground fenugreek**
- **2 medium tomatoes, diced**
- **2 tbsp tomato paste**
- **½ cup chopped fresh coriander**
- **30 large prawn cutlets, deveined and shells removed**
- **1 cup cream**
- **1 quantity Basmati Rice (see page 114)**
- **Salt and red chilli powder to taste**
- **Chopped fresh coriander to garnish (optional)**

Heat oil in a large pan over a low heat and add carom seeds, cardamom, cloves and cinnamon. Cook until you start to smell the aromas of the spices coming through.

Add onion, stirring continuously so it doesn't stick to bottom of pan. Cook until almost brown.

Stir in garlic and ginger and cook until softened and browned. Add turmeric, garam masala, salt and fenugreek and continue cooking until you start to smell the spice aromas.

Stir through tomato and cook until you start to see oil separating from onion and spice mixture. Be sure to take your time with this and keep stirring so that it does not stick to bottom of pan. The mix that you are making is called a Tarka.

Add tomato paste, coriander and prawns and cook until prawns are fully heated through and start to curl (about 5 minutes). Turn heat down low and stir through cream. Slowly increase heat so that cream does not curdle.

Mix cooked rice through prawn mixture. The rice needs to combine with the prawn mixture and should turn into the colour of the mix. Cook until rice is fully heated.

Season to taste with salt and chilli powder.

Garnish with chopped fresh coriander if wished.

BENGALI FISH

Bengali Fish is an East Indian specialty. It has a thin gravy which is light and fragrant. It goes really well with our Mixed Vegetable Pulao (see page 118).

SERVES 6

- 3 tbsp canola oil
- 1 tsp carom seeds
- 1 onion, finely diced
- 1 tbsp crushed fresh garlic
- 1 tbsp crushed fresh ginger
- 1 tsp ground turmeric
- 1½ tsp garam masala
- 1 tsp salt
- 3 medium tomatoes, diced
- 2 tbsp tomato paste
- 500g gurnard fillets, deboned and cut into large chunks
- 2 tbsp plain unsweetened yoghurt
- ½ cup chopped fresh coriander
- 1½ cup boiling water
- Salt and red chilli powder to taste
- Chopped fresh coriander to garnish (optional)

Heat oil in a large pan over a low heat and add carom seeds. Cook until you start to smell the aroma of the carom seeds coming through.

Add onion, stirring continuously so it doesn't stick to bottom of pan. Cook until almost brown.

Stir in garlic and ginger and cook through. Add turmeric, garam masala and salt and continue cooking until you start to smell the spice aromas.

Stir through tomato and tomato paste and keep cooking until you start to see oil separating from onion and spice mixture. Be sure to take your time with this and keep stirring so that it does not stick to bottom of pan. The mix that you are making is called a Tarka.

Add gurnard, yoghurt and coriander and stir through the Tarka. Carefully pour in boiling water and cook for about 10 minutes until yoghurt and water come together and sauce begins to bubble and thicken. Oil will also come to the surface when this is cooked.

Season to taste with salt and chilli powder. Garnish with chopped fresh coriander if wished.

VEGETARIAN MAINS

DAAL MAKHANI

Daal Makhani is a really special dish. It is one of those dishes that, if made with time and love, can become so addictive you cannot stop eating it. Traditionally made on an open fire and cooked overnight, this dish is never missing from the menu at any special occasion in North India. Prepare the beans the day before as they need to soak overnight.

SERVES 6

- 1 cup split black beans
- ⅓ cup red kidney beans
- 1½ tsp salt
- 1 tbsp canola oil
- 2 tbsp clarified butter
- 1 onion, finely diced
- 1 tbsp crushed fresh garlic
- 1 tbsp crushed fresh ginger
- 2 tsp ground turmeric
- 1½ tsp garam masala
- 1 tsp salt
- 1 tsp ground fenugreek
- 2 medium tomatoes, diced
- ¼ cup cream
- ½ cup boiling water
- Salt and red chilli powder to taste
- Finely sliced tomato or chopped fresh coriander to garnish

Put black beans and kidney beans in a bowl and fill with enough water to just cover top of beans. With your hands, mix beans through the water. The water will change colour. Strain water from beans and repeat until water is clear when you mix it. Cover bowl and leave to soak overnight. Remove cover from beans and repeat same process of cleaning beans until water runs clear. Strain.

Place beans in a pressure cooker with 5 cups water and salt. Cook beans until you hear eight whistles or releases of air pressure. You should be able to squash beans between your fingers. Do not strain.

Heat oil and clarified butter in a large pan. Add onion, stirring continuously so it doesn't stick to bottom of pan. Cook until almost brown. Stir in garlic and ginger and cook until softened and browned. Add turmeric, garam masala, salt and fenugreek and cook until you start to smell the spice aromas.

Stir through tomato and cook until you start to see oil separating from onion and spice mixture. Be sure to take your time with this and keep stirring so that it does not stick to bottom of pan. The mix that you are making is called a Tarka.

Add beans and liquid from the pressure cooker to the pan. Cook until mixture starts to come together. Once this is done, turn heat down low and stir through cream. Slowly increase heat so that cream does not curdle.

Carefully pour in boiling water and cook until water and cream come together (about 10 minutes) and sauce begins to bubble and thicken.

Season to taste with salt and chilli powder. Garnish with finely sliced tomato or chopped fresh coriander.

TARKA DAAL

Tarka Daal is the simplest of daals to prepare. It is a staple of the North Indian diet and will appear at most home-cooked meals. You can use a variety of different pulses with this recipe to give different flavours every time.

SERVES 6

- 1½ cups yellow split peas
- 1 tsp salt
- 1 tsp ground turmeric
- 3 tbsp canola oil
- 1 onion, finely diced
- ½ tbsp crushed fresh garlic
- 1 tbsp crushed fresh ginger
- 1 tsp ground turmeric
- 1½ tsp garam masala
- 1 tsp salt
- 3 medium tomatoes, diced
- ¼ cup chopped fresh coriander
- 1 cup boiling water
- Salt and red chilli powder to taste
- Chopped fresh coriander to garnish (optional)

Put split peas in a bowl and fill bowl with enough water to just cover top of peas. With your hands, mix split peas through water. The water will go a cloudy colour. Strain water from split peas and repeat until water is clear when you mix it. Cover bowl and leave to soak for at least 1 hour. This process is cleaning and softening the split peas so that they are just right before you cook them.

Remove cover from split peas and strain. Place split peas in a pot with 5 cups of water, and first measure of salt and turmeric. Bring split peas to the boil and cook until they are soft enough that you can squash them between your fingers. Do not strain.

Heat oil in a large pan over a medium heat. Add onion, stirring continuously so it doesn't stick to bottom of pan. Cook until almost brown.

Stir in garlic and ginger and cook until softened and browned. Add second measure of turmeric, garam masala and second measure of salt and cook until you start to smell the spice aromas.

Stir through tomato and keep cooking until you start to see oil separating from onion and spice mixture. Be sure to take your time with this and keep stirring so that it does not stick to bottom of pan. The mix that you are making is called a Tarka.

Add cooked split peas and liquid from pot to Tarka. Cook until mixture starts to come together and thicken. Add fresh coriander and boiling water and cook until the daal begins to bubble and thicken.

Season to taste with salt and chilli powder. Garnish with chopped fresh coriander if wished.

ALOO GOBI

Aloo Gobi is a drier dish with potatoes, florets of cauliflower, cumin seeds, turmeric and diced tomatoes. After Aloo Gobi was featured in the movie *Bend It Like Beckham*, it became a lot more popular at our restaurants as everyone wanted to try it. It has been one of our most popular vegetarian dishes ever since.

SERVES 6

- 3 tbsp canola oil
- 1½ tsp cumin seeds
- 1 onion, finely diced
- 1 tbsp crushed fresh garlic
- 1 tbsp crushed fresh ginger
- 2 tsp ground turmeric
- 1½ tsp garam masala
- 1 tsp salt
- 2 medium tomatoes, diced
- 1 green chilli, seeded and finely chopped (optional)
- 6 medium Agria potatoes, peeled, cut into 2cm x 2cm cubes and boiled until tender
- ½ cauliflower, cut into florets and boiled until al dente
- ¼ cup chopped fresh coriander
- Salt and red chilli powder to taste
- Chopped fresh coriander to garnish (optional)

Heat oil in a large pan over a low heat. Add cumin seeds and cook until you start to smell the aroma of the spice coming through.

Add onion, stirring continuously so it doesn't stick to bottom of pan. Cook until almost brown.

Stir in garlic and ginger and cook until browned and softened. Add turmeric, garam masala and salt and continue cooking until you start to smell the spice aromas.

Stir through tomato and green chilli (if using) and keep cooking until you start to see oil separating from onion and spice mixture. Be sure to take your time with this and keep stirring so that it does not stick to bottom of pan. The mix that you are making is called a Tarka.

Stir potato and cauliflower through the Tarka and add coriander. Cook until potato and cauliflower are soft enough that a knife can slide through them easily.

Season to taste with salt and chilli powder. Garnish with chopped fresh coriander if wished.

MATTAR PANEER

Mattar Paneer is an interesting combination of peas and paneer. The spices in this dish infuse the paneer with a beautiful flavour. This dish goes well with Tarka Daal (see page 94) and Roti (see page 124).

SERVES 6

- 3 tbsp canola oil
- 2 tsp cumin seeds
- 1 onion, finely diced
- 1 tbsp crushed fresh garlic
- 1 tbsp crushed fresh ginger
- 1 tsp ground turmeric
- 1½ tsp garam masala
- 1 tsp salt
- 1 tsp ground fenugreek
- 3 medium tomatoes, diced
- 2 tbsp tomato paste
- 2 cups cold water
- 400g paneer cut into 4cm x 4cm cubes (see page 24)
- 1 cup frozen peas
- ½ cup chopped fresh coriander
- ¼ cup cream
- Salt and red chilli powder to taste
- Chopped fresh coriander to garnish (optional)

Heat oil in a large pan over a low heat. Add cumin seeds and cook until you start to smell the aroma of the cumin coming through.

Add onion, stirring continuously so it doesn't stick to bottom of pan. Cook until almost brown.

Stir in garlic and ginger and cook until softened and browned. Add turmeric, garam masala, salt and fenugreek and continue cooking until you start to smell the spice aromas.

Stir through tomato and keep cooking until you start to see oil separating from onion and spice mixture. Add tomato paste and cook through so it all comes together. Be sure to take your time with this and keep stirring so that it does not stick to bottom of pan. The mix that you are making is called a Tarka.

Add cold water and stir through the Tarka until it is fully combined. Add cubed paneer, peas and coriander and cook until the paneer is heated through and peas soften. Add cream and stir through.

Season to taste with salt and chilli powder. Garnish with chopped fresh coriander.

AMRITSARI CHOLE

Chole was made famous on the side streets of Amritsar where they have perfected the flavours of this dish. There are eateries in Amritsar that only sell this dish and have big queues waiting to get a taste. Amritsari Chole is traditionally served with Bhatura (fried bread), chopped onion and green chilli. Prepare the chickpeas the day before as they need to soak overnight. If you don't have a pressure cooker you can replace the dried chickpeas with tinned chickpeas and skip the soaking and pressure cooker process.

SERVES 6

- 2 cups dried chickpeas
- 1 black cardamom pod
- 1 tsp salt
- 3 tbsp canola oil
- 1 onion, finely diced
- 1 tbsp crushed fresh garlic
- 1 tbsp crushed fresh ginger
- 1 tsp ground turmeric
- 1½ tsp garam masala
- 1 tsp salt
- 1 tsp ground fenugreek
- 3 medium tomatoes, diced
- ½ cup tomato purée
- 1 cup chopped fresh coriander
- 2 cups cold water
- ½ tbsp chana masala (see page 18)
- Salt and red chilli powder to taste
- Chopped fresh coriander and diced red or white onion to garnish (optional)

Place chickpeas in a bowl and fill bowl with enough water to just cover top of chickpeas. With your hands, mix chickpeas through water. Strain water from chickpeas. Cover chickpeas again with water. Add black cardamom pod, cover bowl and leave to soak overnight. Remove cover from chickpeas and strain.

Place strained chickpeas in a pressure cooker with 5 cups water and salt. Cook chickpeas until you hear five whistles or releases of air pressure. The chickpeas should be soft enough that you can squash them between your fingers. Strain chickpeas, leaving in the black cardamom pod.

Heat oil in a large pan over a low heat. Add onion, stirring continuously so it doesn't stick to bottom of pan. Cook until almost brown. Stir in garlic and ginger and cook until softened and browned. Add turmeric, garam masala, salt and fenugreek and continue cooking until you start to smell the spice aromas.

Stir through tomato and keep cooking until you start to see oil separating from onion and spice mixture. Add tomato purée and mix through until combined. Be sure to take your time with this and keep stirring so that it does not stick to bottom of pan. The mix that you are making is called a Tarka.

Mix chickpeas into Tarka until they are heated through. Add water and cook for about 10 minutes. Stir through fresh coriander and chana masala. Cook for a further 2 minutes.

Season to taste with salt and chilli powder. Garnish with chopped fresh coriander and diced red or white onion if wished.

PANEER SHIMLA MIRCH

Paneer Shimla Mirch is a lively vegetarian dish. It has a beautiful mix of colours and flavours. The textures of the soft paneer and the crunchy capsicums make this dish a real crowd-pleaser.

SERVES 6

- 3 tbsp canola oil
- 2 tsp cumin seeds
- 2 sticks cinnamon (about 5cm long)
- 4 small bay leaves
- 1 onion, finely diced
- 1 tbsp crushed fresh garlic
- 1 tbsp crushed fresh ginger
- 2 tsp ground turmeric
- 1½ tsp garam masala
- 1 tsp salt
- 1 tbsp ground fenugreek
- ½ tsp ground coriander
- 3 medium tomatoes, diced
- 3 tbsp tomato paste
- 1 onion, thinly sliced
- ½ red capsicum, cut julienne style
- ½ green capsicum, cut julienne style
- ½ cup cold water
- 400g paneer, cut into 2cm x 2cm cubes (see page 24)
- ½ cup chopped fresh coriander
- Salt and red chilli powder to taste
- Chopped fresh coriander to garnish (optional)

Heat oil in a large pan over a low heat. Add cumin seeds, cinnamon sticks and bay leaves. Cook over a low heat until you start to smell the aromas of the spices coming through.

Add diced onion, stirring continuously so it doesn't stick to bottom of pan. Cook until almost brown.

Stir in garlic and ginger and cook until softened and browned. Add turmeric, garam masala, salt, fenugreek and ground coriander and continue cooking until you start to smell the spice aromas.

Stir through tomato and tomato paste and cook until you start to see oil separating from onion and spice mixture.

Add thinly sliced onion and capsicums and fry until onion and capsicum begin to soften and tomato paste is mixed through. Be sure to take your time with this and keep stirring so that it does not stick to bottom of pan.

Add cold water and stir through the capsicum mix until fully combined. Add cubed paneer and coriander and cook until paneer is heated through (about 5 minutes).

Season to taste with salt and chilli powder. Garnish with chopped fresh coriander if wished.

PALAK PANEER

Palak Paneer is a mix of home-made Indian cheese and spinach. This is an all-time favourite of our vegetarian customers.

SERVES 6

- 4 bunches spinach, chopped
- 3 tbsp canola oil
- 1 tsp cumin seeds
- 1 onion, finely diced
- 1 tbsp crushed fresh garlic
- 1 tbsp crushed fresh ginger
- 1 tsp ground turmeric
- 1½ tsp garam masala
- 1 tsp salt
- 3 medium tomatoes, diced
- ½ cup cream
- 400g paneer, cut into 2cm x 2cm cubes (see page 24)
- Salt and red chilli powder to taste
- Chopped fresh coriander to garnish (optional)

Place spinach in a pot and fill with just enough water to cover spinach. Cook until spinach softens (about 10 minutes). It is important not to cook this for too long.

Strain water from softened spinach. Put spinach in a blender and process to a smooth paste.

Heat oil in a large pan over a medium heat. Add cumin seeds. Cook until you start to smell the aroma of the spice coming through. Add onion, stirring continuously so it doesn't stick to bottom of pan. Cook until almost brown.

Stir in garlic and ginger and cook until softened and browned. Add turmeric, garam masala and salt and continue cooking until you start to smell the spice aromas.

Stir through tomato and keep cooking until you start to see oil separating from onion and spice mixture. Be sure to take your time with this and keep stirring so that it does not stick to bottom of pan. The mix that you are making is called a Tarka.

Add spinach paste and cook until the spinach is fully heated through. Turn heat down low and stir through cream. Slowly increase heat so that cream does not curdle.

Add cubed paneer and cook until paneer is heated through and softens (about 5 minutes).

Season to taste with salt and chilli powder. Garnish with chopped fresh coriander if wished.

GANGA JAMUNA SUBZI

This is a mixed vegetable dish. Its name derives from two Indian rivers (Ganga and Yamuna) that meet together. This dish was given its name by our grandfather, Jasbir Singh Gill.

SERVES 6

- 1 carrot, sliced into rounds
- ½ cauliflower, cut into florets
- 150g green beans, cut into 2cm pieces
- 3 tbsp canola oil
- 1 tsp cumin seeds
- 1 onion, finely diced
- 1 tbsp crushed fresh garlic
- 1 tbsp crushed fresh ginger
- 2 tsp ground turmeric
- 1½ tsp garam masala
- 1 tsp salt
- 1 tsp ground fenugreek
- 3 medium tomatoes, diced
- 1 courgette, sliced into rounds
- 1 medium Agria potato, peeled and boiled until soft, then cut into 2cm x 2cm cubes
- 1 cup frozen green peas
- ½ cup chopped fresh coriander
- ¼ cup cream
- Salt and red chilli powder to taste
- Chopped fresh coriander to garnish

Place carrot, cauliflower and green beans in a pot with some water and boil until they soften. Strain and set aside.

Heat oil in a large pan over a low heat. Add cumin seeds and cook until you start to smell the cumin aroma coming through.

Add onion, stirring continuously so it doesn't stick to bottom of pan. Cook until almost brown.

Stir in garlic and ginger and cook until softened and browned. Add turmeric, garam masala, salt and fenugreek and cook until you start to smell the spice aromas.

Stir through tomato and keep cooking until you start to see oil separating from onion and spice mixture. Be sure to take your time with this and keep stirring so that it does not stick to bottom of pan. The mix that you are making is called a Tarka.

Mix carrot, cauliflower, green beans, courgette, potato and peas through the Tarka until they are heated through and soft. Add coriander and stir through. Turn heat down and stir through cream. Increase heat slowly so that cream does not curdle. Cook until cream has combined with the dish (about 5 minutes).

Season to taste with salt and chilli powder. Garnish with chopped fresh coriander.

MALAI KOFTA

Malai Kofta has a velvety, creamy gravy flavoured with cardamom and thickened with cashew nuts. The gravy is complemented by our koftas made from a comforting combination of paneer, potatoes, breadcrumbs and warm spices.

SERVES 6

- 4 medium Agria potatoes, peeled and boiled until tender
- 200g paneer (see page 24)
- 1 tsp salt
- ¼ tsp ground white pepper
- ½ cup chopped fresh coriander
- ¼ cup fine breadcrumbs
- 50g sultanas
- Canola oil for frying
- 4 green cardamom pods
- 4 cloves
- 2 bay leaves
- 1 onion, puréed to a fine consistency
- 1 tbsp each crushed garlic and ginger
- 1 tsp ground turmeric
- 1½ tsp garam masala
- 1 tsp salt
- 1 tsp ground fenugreek
- 2 medium tomatoes, diced
- 3 tbsp tomato paste
- 1½ cups cream
- 2 tbsp finely crushed cashew nuts
- Salt and red chilli powder to taste
- Chopped fresh coriander and crushed cashew nuts to garnish (optional)

Grate potatoes and paneer into a mixing bowl. Add salt, white pepper, coriander and breadcrumbs and mix through with your hands until everything comes together. Roll mixture into small balls and press a couple of sultanas into centre of each ball.

Make sure oil is hot enough to fry balls by dropping a small piece of the kofta mix into the oil. If it rises to the top, the oil is ready. Fry balls until golden brown (about 5 minutes). It is best to only do about five balls at a time. Once balls are cooked, place on a paper towel and set aside.

Heat 3 tablespoons canola oil in a large pan over a low heat. Add cardamom pods, cloves and bay leaves and simmer until you start to smell the spice aromas. Add onion, stirring continuously so it doesn't stick to bottom of pan. Cook until almost brown.

Stir in garlic and ginger and cook until softened and browned. Add turmeric, garam masala, salt and fenugreek and cook until you start to smell the spice aromas.

Stir through tomato and keep cooking until you start to see oil separating from onion and spice mixture. Be sure to take your time with this and keep stirring so that it does not stick to bottom of pan. The mix that you are making is called a Tarka.

Add tomato paste and cook until it has combined with the Tarka. Turn heat down low and stir through cream. Slowly increase heat so cream does not curdle. Mix through cashew nuts.

Carefully pour in 1 cup boiling water and cook until water and cream come together and sauce begins to bubble. Season to taste with salt and chilli powder. Place kofta balls in sauce and heat through. This will not take very long.

Garnish with chopped fresh coriander and crushed cashew nuts if wished.

ALOO BAINGAN

Aloo Baingan is a dry dish with hearty flavours. The chaat masala and lemon juice that are added to the dish give it a nice zingy flavour. Aloo Baingan is a great winter dish and we consider it comfort food.

SERVES 6

- 3 tbsp canola oil
- 2 tsp cumin seeds
- 1 onion, finely diced
- 1 tbsp crushed fresh garlic
- 1 tbsp crushed fresh ginger
- 1 tsp ground turmeric
- 1½ tsp garam masala
- 1 tsp salt
- 1 tsp ground fenugreek
- 1 tbsp canola oil
- 200g eggplant, cut into 2cm x 2cm cubes
- 3 medium tomatoes, diced
- 2 tbsp tomato paste
- 2 medium Agria potatoes, boiled and cut into 2cm x 2cm cubes
- ¼ cup cold water
- ½ cup chopped fresh coriander
- ½ tsp chaat masala
- 1 tbsp lemon juice
- Salt and red chilli powder to taste
- Chopped fresh coriander to garnish

Heat first measure of oil in a large pan over a low heat. Add cumin seeds and cook until you start to smell the aroma of the spice coming through.

Add onion, stirring continuously so it doesn't stick to bottom of pan. Cook until almost brown.

Stir in garlic and ginger and cook until browned and softened. Add turmeric, garam masala, salt and fenugreek and cook until you start to smell the spice aromas. Add second measure of oil and eggplant. Fry until eggplant is softened.

Stir through tomato and keep cooking until you start to see oil separating from mixture. Add tomato paste and cook through so it all comes together. Be sure to take your time with this and keep stirring so that it does not stick to bottom of pan.

Add potato and cook mixture until soft. Pour in cold water and stir through until fully combined. Add coriander and cook until mixture is fully heated. Stir through chaat masala and lemon juice.

Season to taste with salt and chilli powder. Garnish with chopped fresh coriander.

RICE

BASMATI RICE

In India basmati rice is considered the king of all rice. It is grown in the Punjab region of India and also in Pakistan. Basmati is a long-grain rice and when cooked it is light and fluffy with a fragrant aroma.

SERVES 6

- **2 cups long-grain basmati rice**
- **1 tbsp lemon juice**
- **1 tsp canola oil**
- **3 bay leaves**

Put rice in a bowl and cover with water. Leave to soak for at least 30 minutes.

Mix rice through with your hands and then strain. Add more water, mix and strain again. Repeat this process at least three times to wash the rice.

Put cleaned rice into a medium pot with 4 cups water, lemon juice, oil and bay leaves.

Place a lid on pot and cook over a high heat until water comes to a boil then reduce heat to a simmer. Do not remove the lid or stir rice throughout this process. You will see that the water will reduce. Once there appears to be no water left, remove the lid, take a fork and bring rice from bottom of pot to top. You will notice that there will still be some water and rice is more cooked at bottom of pot. Once rice is mixed, put lid back on and continue to cook over a medium heat until no water remains. You should be left with nice fluffy rice that is not sticky.

KASHMIRI PULAO

If you are looking for a slightly sweet bite to your rice, Kashmiri Pulao is the answer. The sweetness of coconut and sultanas combines beautifully with the savoury flavour of the nuts. Kashmiri Pulao goes really well with our Chicken Korma (see page 54).

SERVES 6

- **2 tbsp canola oil**
- **2 tsp paprika**
- **2 tbsp canola oil**
- **¼ cup slivered almonds**
- **¼ cup roughly chopped cashew nuts**
- **1 quantity Basmati Rice (see page 114)**
- **½ cup sultanas**
- **½ cup desiccated coconut**
- **¼ cup fresh chopped coriander**
- **Salt to taste**

Heat first measure of oil in a small pan over a low heat. Add paprika and mix through until oil becomes a dark red colour. Make sure you do not burn paprika. Once oil has changed colour, remove from heat and strain oil to separate it from paprika grains. Leave oil to cool.

Heat second measure of oil in a large pan over a low heat and add almonds and cashew nuts. Toast on a low heat until they brown.

Mix rice into pan with nuts. Add sultanas and paprika oil and mix through until the colour of the rice changes. Add desiccated coconut, coriander and salt to taste. Mix through. You will not need to cook this for long as rice is already cooked.

Once all ingredients are mixed evenly through rice, remove from heat and serve.

MIXED VEGETABLE PULAO

Mixed Vegetable Pulao is very attractive to the eye with its mix of yellow rice, green beans and orange carrots. It goes very well with all our dishes with rich gravies.

SERVES 6

- **2 tbsp canola oil**
- **1 tsp cumin seeds**
- **½ carrot, cut into 2cm x 2cm cubes**
- **½ courgette, cut into 2cm x 2cm cubes**
- **100g green beans, cut into 2cm pieces**
- **½ cup frozen green peas**
- **1 tsp ground turmeric**
- **1 tsp salt**
- **½ tsp ground white pepper**
- **1 quantity Basmati Rice (see page 114)**

Heat oil in a large pan over a low heat and add cumin seeds. Stir seeds until you start to smell the spice aroma.

Add carrot, courgette and beans and sauté. Do not let the vegetables soften too much. Add peas, turmeric, salt and white pepper and stir through.

Mix rice into pan with vegetables. You will not need to cook this for long as rice is already cooked. Once vegetables are mixed evenly through rice, remove from heat and serve.

PEAS PULAO

Peas Pulao is the most common pulao cooked in North Indian homes. It is an unfussy dish so is therefore great in combination with other dishes that have more intense punch.

SERVES 6

- 2 tbsp canola oil
- 1 tsp cumin seeds
- ½ onion, thinly sliced
- 1 cup frozen green peas
- 1 tsp salt
- ½ tsp ground white pepper
- 1 quantity Basmati Rice (see page 114)

Heat oil in a large pan over a low heat and add cumin seeds. Stir seeds until you start to smell the spice aroma.

Add onion, peas, salt and white pepper and sauté. You do not want onion to soften too much.

Mix rice into pan with vegetables. You will not need to cook this for long as rice is already cooked.

Once onion and peas are mixed evenly through rice, remove from heat and serve.

BREADS

ROTI

Roti is a staple of the North Indian diet. It is eaten with all meals and goes well with any curry. There are different varieties of roti and we have shown a few versions in the following recipes.

SERVES 6

2 cups wholemeal flour
1 tsp salt
2 cups lukewarm water
1 tsp canola oil
Flour for dusting
Canola oil for drizzling

Place flour, salt and water in a large mixing bowl and knead together with your hands. You may need to add a little extra water to the dough but only add if needed as dough should remain firm.

Just as dough is about to combine, add oil and mix dough into a large smooth ball. The dough should not stick to your fingers.

Break off some dough and roll into a ball slightly larger than a golf ball. Flatten ball with your palms.

Dust a clean surface with flour and place flattened ball on it. Roll out dough into a circle about 15cm in diameter and 1.5mm thick.

Repeat until you have made as many rotis as you require. Any leftover dough can be kept in the refrigerator for up to three days.

Place a flat frying pan over a high heat. Put your rolled roti onto the hot pan with no oil. Lightly cook on both sides for about 2 minutes. Drizzle top of roti with oil, flip it over and cook until golden brown. Repeat on other side so both sides are golden brown.

ONION KULCHA

Onion Kulcha is made with wholemeal flour and a tasty mix of onion and spices. It can accompany a meal or can be eaten on its own with Indian pickle and yoghurt.

SERVES 6

ROTI

- 2 cups wholemeal flour
- 1 tsp salt
- 2 cups lukewarm water
- 1 tsp canola oil

ONION MIX

- 1 onion, finely diced
- ½ tsp salt
- ½ tsp carom seeds
- 1 tbsp chopped fresh coriander
- 2 tsp crushed ginger
- Red chilli powder to taste
- 2 green chillies, finely chopped (optional)

- Flour for dusting
- Canola oil for drizzling

Place flour, first measure of salt and water in a large mixing bowl and knead together with your hands. You may need to add a little extra water to the dough but only add if needed as dough should remain firm.

Just as dough is about to combine, add oil and mix dough into a large smooth ball. The dough should not stick to your fingers.

Combine onion, second measure of salt, carom seeds, coriander, ginger, chilli powder to taste and chillies (if using) in a bowl and mix together with your fingers.

Break off some dough and roll into a ball slightly larger than a golf ball. Flatten ball with your palms. Place 2 tablespoons of onion mix in centre of flattened dough ball. Take sides of dough and wrap over onion mix. Roll into a ball again and flatten in your palms so that onion mix has spread evenly through middle of dough all the way to sides.

Dust a clean surface with flour and place flattened ball on it. Roll out dough into a circle about 15cm in diameter and 2mm thick.

Repeat until you have made as many kulchas as you require. Any leftover dough can be kept in the refrigerator for up to three days.

Place a flat frying pan over a high heat. Put your rolled kulcha onto the hot pan with no oil. Lightly cook on both sides (about 2 minutes). Drizzle top of kulcha with oil, flip it over and cook until golden brown. Repeat on other side so both sides are golden brown.

PANEER KULCHA

Paneer Kulcha is made with wholemeal flour, paneer and spices. It is delicious to eat with a meal or can be eaten on its own with Indian pickle and yoghurt.

SERVES 6

ROTI

- 2 cups wholemeal flour
- 1 tsp salt
- 2 cups lukewarm water
- 1 tsp canola oil

PANEER MIX

- 300g paneer (see page 24)
- ¼ onion, finely diced
- 1 tsp salt
- 1 tsp cumin seeds
- 1 tbsp chopped fresh coriander
- 2 tsp crushed ginger
- ¼ tsp garam masala
- Red chilli powder to taste
- 2 green chillies, finely chopped (optional)

- Flour for dusting
- Canola oil for drizzling

Place flour, first measure of salt and water in a large mixing bowl and knead together with your hands. You may need to add a little extra water to the dough but only add if needed as dough should remain firm.

Just as dough is about to combine, add oil and mix dough into a large smooth ball. The dough should not stick to your fingers.

Grate paneer into a bowl and add onion, second measure of salt, cumin seeds, coriander, ginger, garam masala, chilli powder to taste and chillies (if using). Mix together with your fingers.

Break off some dough and roll into a ball slightly larger than a golf ball. Flatten ball with your palms. Place 2 tablespoons of paneer mix in centre of flattened dough ball. Take sides of dough and wrap over paneer mix. Roll into a ball again and flatten in your palms so that paneer mix has spread evenly through middle of dough all the way to sides.

Dust a clean surface with flour and place flattened ball on it. Roll out dough into a circle about 15cm in diameter and 2mm thick.

Repeat until you have made as many kulchas as you require. Any leftover dough can be kept in the refrigerator for up to three days.

Place a flat frying pan over a high heat. Put your rolled kulcha onto the hot pan with no oil. Lightly cook on both sides (about 2 minutes). Drizzle top of kulcha with oil, flip it over and cook until golden brown. Repeat on other side so both sides are golden brown.

NAAN

Naan is normally cooked in the tandoor. The recipe below gives you the same sort of flavour and look as using a tandoor by using your oven. We have also given a variation for Garlic Naan.

SERVES 6

- **3 cups plain flour**
- **1 tsp salt**
- **1 tsp sugar**
- **1 tsp baking powder**
- **1 egg**
- **1 cup milk**
- **Flour for dusting**
- **1 tbsp canola oil (for Garlic Naan)**
- **½ tbsp crushed fresh garlic (for Garlic Naan)**

Preheat oven to 220°C fan bake. Line a baking tray with baking paper.

Place flour, salt, sugar and baking powder in a large mixing bowl and stir together. Make a well in the middle and crack egg into well.

Gradually add milk to flour and egg until dough combines into a sticky consistency. The dough will stick to your hands.

Dust a clean surface with flour and roll dough through it so it becomes less sticky and you are able to divide it into 12 even balls. Leave balls to rest for 30 minutes.

Dip a ball into flour and then roll out into an oval shape on a board sprinkled with flour to prevent dough from sticking. Repeat with remaining balls of dough. Place on lined baking tray.

If you are making Garlic Naan, mix oil and garlic together and brush evenly over naan.

Place naan in oven. They will take about 3–4 minutes to cook. It is best to keep an eye on them. When you see bubbles form and turn golden brown, it is time to remove naan from oven.

ALOO PARANTHA

This is a traditional Indian breakfast dish. In modern times it is served as a Sunday brunch normally with a Lassi and spiced scrambled egg. A Punjabi household favourite.

SERVES 6

ROTI

- 2 cups wholemeal flour
- 1 tsp salt
- 2 cups lukewarm water
- 1 tsp canola oil

POTATO MIX

- 2 medium Agria potatoes, peeled and boiled until soft
- ¼ onion, finely diced
- 1 tsp salt
- 1 tsp cumin seeds
- 1 tbsp chopped fresh coriander
- 2 tsp crushed ginger
- 1 tsp ground turmeric
- Red chilli powder to taste
- 2 green chillies, finely chopped (optional)

- Flour for dusting
- Canola oil for drizzling

Place flour, salt and water in a large mixing bowl and knead together with your hands. You may need to add a little extra water to the dough but only add if needed as dough should remain firm.

Just as dough is about to combine, add oil and mix dough into a large smooth ball. The dough should not stick to your fingers.

In a bowl, mash potatoes with your hands and add remaining potato mix ingredients. Stir together with your fingers.

Break off some dough and roll into a ball slightly larger than a golf ball. Flatten ball with your palms. Place 2 tablespoons of potato mix in centre of flattened dough ball. Take sides of dough and wrap over potato mix. Roll into a ball again and flatten in your palms so that potato mix has spread evenly through middle of dough all the way to sides.

Dust a clean surface with flour and place flattened ball on it. Roll out dough into a circle about 18cm in diameter and 3–4mm thick.

Repeat until you have made as many paranthas as you require. Any leftover dough can be kept in the refrigerator for up to three days.

Place a flat frying pan over a high heat. Put a rolled parantha onto the hot pan with no oil. Lightly cook on both sides (about 2 minutes). Drizzle top of parantha with oil, flip it over and cook until golden brown. Repeat on other side so both sides are golden brown.

LACHA PARANTHA

Lacha Parantha is a decadent bread layered with clarified butter and sprinkled with fenugreek. This bread goes well with our non-creamy dishes.

SERVES 6

- 2 cups wholemeal flour
- 1 tsp salt
- 2 cups lukewarm water
- 1 tsp canola oil
- Flour for dusting
- Clarified butter to brush on paranthas
- 1 tsp ground fenugreek
- Canola oil for drizzling

Place flour, salt and water in a large mixing bowl and knead together with your hands. You may need to add a little extra water to the dough but only add if needed as dough should remain firm.

Just as dough is about to combine, add oil and mix dough into a large smooth ball. The dough should not stick to your fingers.

Break off some dough and roll into a ball slightly larger than a golf ball. Flatten ball with your palms.

Dust a clean surface with flour and place flattened ball on it. Roll out ball into a circle about 15cm in diameter and 2mm thick.

Generously brush with clarified butter then fold each side into centre, like an envelope (four sides). Sprinkle fenugreek over top and roll again to a circle 15cm in diameter and 2mm thick.

Repeat until you have made as many lacha paranthas as you require. Any leftover dough can be kept in the refrigerator for up to three days.

Place a flat frying pan over a high heat. Put a rolled lacha parantha onto the hot pan with no oil. Lightly cook on both sides for about 2 minutes. Drizzle top of parantha with oil, flip it over and cook until golden brown. Repeat on other side so both sides are golden brown.

ACCOMPANIMENTS

RAITA

Raita is a great side to go with spicy dishes. The yoghurt and cucumber give a cooling effect to balance out the palate.

SERVES 6

- 750g plain unsweetened yoghurt
- ½ large telegraph cucumber
- 1 tsp salt
- 1 tsp ground cumin
- Chopped fresh coriander to garnish
- Ground cumin to garnish

Place yoghurt in a bowl and whisk to a smooth consistency.

Grate cucumber and add to yoghurt.

Mix through salt and cumin.

Garnish with chopped fresh coriander and ground cumin.

LITTLE INDIA CHILLI CHUTNEY

Our chilli chutney was born out of a particular customer's demand for something extremely hot. No matter what we gave him he was not satisfied. Sukhmohan decided it was time to blow his socks off. Needless to say that customer, and many customers since then, have been more than satisfied. Sometimes too satisfied!

SERVES 6

- 6 tbsp canola oil
- 1 onion, puréed
- 1 tbsp crushed fresh ginger
- 1 tbsp crushed fresh garlic
- 2 green chillies, finely diced
- ½ tsp salt
- ¼ tsp ground white pepper
- 1 tsp ground fenugreek
- ¼ tsp garam masala
- 1 tsp ground turmeric
- 4 dried red chillies, ground
- 1 tbsp red chilli powder
- 1 tbsp vinegar
- 1 tbsp tomato paste

Heat oil in a medium pan over a medium heat. Add onion, stirring continuously so it doesn't stick to bottom of pan. Cook until almost brown.

Stir in ginger, garlic and green chillies and cook until browned and softened. Add salt, white pepper, fenugreek, garam masala, turmeric, red chillies and chilli powder and continue cooking until you can start to smell the spice aromas.

Add vinegar and tomato paste and keep cooking until you start to see oil separating from onion and spice mixture. Be sure to take your time with this and keep stirring so that it does not stick to bottom of pan. You should get a nice film of oil above the onion mix. When this happens, the chilli chutney is ready.

To begin with taste a small amount only as it is hot!

KECHUMBER

Kechumber is a delightful mix of cucumber, tomato and onion combined with lemon juice and chaat masala. It complements all of our starters.

SERVES 6

- **¾ large telegraph cucumber**
- **2 tomatoes**
- **2 red onions**
- **1 tbsp chaat masala**
- **1 tbsp lemon juice**
- **2 green chillies, finely chopped (optional)**

Remove seeds from cucumber and tomatoes and finely dice. Finely dice red onions, discarding the core of the onion.

Combine tomatoes, cucumber and onion in a mixing bowl and add chaat masala and lemon juice. Mix together with your hands.

Taste Kechumber and add more chaat masala or lemon juice according to your taste. If you like it spicy, add chillies.

MINT CHUTNEY

Mint Chutney is a wonderful accompaniment to all our meat and seafood dishes. The combination of mint and green chilli gives a nice fresh zing to the palate.

SERVES 6

- 750g plain unsweetened yoghurt
- 1 bunch mint
- ¼ onion
- 2 green chillies
- 1 tsp salt
- ¼ tsp ground white pepper
- Pinch of red chilli powder
- Salt and red chilli powder to taste

Place yoghurt in a bowl and whisk to a smooth consistency.

Put mint, onion and chillies into a blender and purée to a fine consistency.

Add purée, salt, white pepper and pinch of chilli powder to yoghurt and whisk through. The yoghurt will turn light green in colour.

Season to taste with extra salt and chilli powder.

TAMARIND CHUTNEY

Tamarind Chutney has a sweet yet tangy flavour. This chutney goes really well with all of our vegetarian starters, especially our Vegetable Samosas (see page 38).

SERVES 6

400g wet tamarind
2 cups cold water
1 tsp cumin seeds, roasted
3 tbsp sugar
2 tsp salt
1½ tbsp grated jaggery (see page 23)
1 tsp ground cumin
Pinch of red chilli powder

Break up wet tamarind into medium-sized chunks and put in a large pot. Add cold water and bring to a boil.

Once tamarind is boiling, reduce heat to a simmer. Add cumin seeds, sugar, salt, jaggery, ground cumin and chilli powder. Mix through and continue to simmer until tamarind pulp separates from seeds. It should be a thick consistency.

Pour tamarind into strainer and leave until it cools. Once cool, squeeze tamarind pulp with your hands so liquid and seeds strain into bowl and pulp is left in strainer. Discard liquid and seeds.

Your Tamarind Chutney is now ready. Place in a small dish to serve.

INDEX

PENGUIN BOOKS
Published by the Penguin Group
Penguin Group (NZ), 67 Apollo Drive, Rosedale,
Auckland 0632, New Zealand (a division of Penguin New Zealand Pty Ltd)
Penguin Group (USA) Inc., 375 Hudson Street,
New York, New York 10014, USA
Penguin Group (Canada), 90 Eglinton Avenue East, Suite 700, Toronto,
Ontario, M4P 2Y3, Canada (a division of Penguin Canada Books Inc.)
Penguin Books Ltd, 80 Strand, London, WC2R 0RL, England
Penguin Ireland, 25 St Stephen's Green,
Dublin 2, Ireland (a division of Penguin Books Ltd)
Penguin Group (Australia), 707 Collins Street, Melbourne,
Victoria 3008, Australia (a division of Penguin Australia Pty Ltd)
Penguin Books India Pvt Ltd, 11, Community Centre,
Panchsheel Park, New Delhi – 110 017, India
Penguin Books (South Africa) (Pty) Ltd, Block D, Rosebank Office Park,
181 Jan Smuts Avenue, Parktown North, Gauteng 2193, South Africa
Penguin (Beijing) Ltd 7F, Tower B, Jiaming Center, 27 East Third Ring Road North,
Chaoyang District, Beijing 100020, China

Penguin Books Ltd, Registered Offices: 80 Strand, London, WC2R 0RL, England

First published by Penguin Group (NZ), 2014
10 9 8 7 6 5 4 3 2 1

Designed and typeset by Jenny Haslimeier, © Penguin Group (NZ)
Food styling by Athena Sommerfeld
Images on pages 8–17 and back cover flap supplied by Little India®
Prepress by Image Centre Ltd
Printed in China by South China Printing Company

ISBN 978-0-143-57083-7

A catalogue record for this book is available
from the National Library of New Zealand.

www.penguin.co.nz